# THE FIFTH AMENDMENT

The ★ ★ ★ ★ ★ ★ ★
# AMERICAN
# HERITAGE
# HISTORY *of the*
# BILL *of* RIGHTS

# THE FIFTH
# AMENDMENT

**Burnham Holmes**

Introduction by
## WARREN E. BURGER
Chief Justice of the United States
1969–1986

Silver Burdett Press

*For Vicki*

*Cover:* Among Fifth Amendment rights are the protection against double jeopardy and the protection against forced self-incrimination.

CONSULTANTS:

Robert M. Goldberg
Consultant to Social Studies
  Department
(formerly Department Chair)
Oceanside Middle School
Oceanside, New York

Michael H. Reggio
Law-Related Education
  Coordinator
Oklahoma Bar Association
Oklahoma City, Oklahoma

Herbert Sloan
Assistant Professor of History
Barnard College
New York, New York

Text and Cover Design: Circa 86, Inc.

Copyright © 1991 by Gallin House Press, Inc.
Introduction copyright © 1991 by Silver Burdett Press, Inc.

Published by Silver Burdett Press, Inc., a division of Simon & Schuster, Inc.,
Englewood Cliffs, N.J. 07632.

Library of Congress Cataloging-in-Publication Data

Holmes, Burnham, 1942–
   The Fifth Amendment/by Burnham Holmes: with an introduction
by Warren E. Burger.
   p. cm.—(The American Heritage history of the Bill of
Rights)
   Includes bibliographical references and indexes.
   Summary: Traces the history of the several clauses of the Fifth Amendment: the right to a grand jury, due process, self-incrimination, double jeopardy, and eminent domain.
   1. United States—Constitutional law—Amendments—5th—History—
Juvenile literature. 2. Grand jury—United States—History—
Juvenile literature. 3. Self-incrimination—United States—
History—Juvenile literature. 4. Double jeopardy—United States—
History—Juvenile literature. 5. Due process of law—United
States—History—Juvenile literature. 6. Eminent domain—United
States—History—Juvenile literature. [1. United States—
Constitutional law—Amendments—5th—History. 2. Civil rights—
History.] I. Title. II. Series.
KF4558 5th.H65 1991
345.73'04—dc20
[347.3054]
                                                        90-49593
                                                            CIP
                                                             AC

Manufactured in the United States of America.

ISBN 0-382-24183-5 [lib. bdg.]
10 9 8 7 6 5 4 3 2 1

ISBN 0-382-24196-7 [pbk.]
10 9 8 7 6 5 4 3 2 1

# ONTENTS

# Introduction

## WARREN E. BURGER
*Chief Justice of the United States, 1969–1986*

The Fifth Amendment assures several fundamental protections to persons accused of federal crimes: it protects them against compelled self-incrimination and from potential excesses of law enforcement and entitles them to a hearing before a grand jury. Such safeguards are essential to the American concept of personal liberty. But the concept of freedom and liberty is much broader than that.

Concepts of liberty—the values liberty protects—inspired the Framers of our Constitution and the Bill of Rights to some of their most impassioned eloquence. "Liberty, the greatest of earthly possessions—give us that precious jewel, and you may take everything else," declaimed Patrick Henry. Those toilers in the "vineyard of liberty" sensed the historic nature of their mission, and their foresight accounts for the survival of the Bill of Rights.

The Fifth Amendment provides the first principles for a code of criminal legal procedure that directly involves all Americans, whether private citizens or officers of the courts. The so-called Miranda rights are familiar to viewers of television crime dramas, and those citizens who work in law enforcement must be vigilant to assure them.

The long-term success of the system of ordered liberty set up by our Constitution was by no means foreordained. The bicentennial of the Bill of Rights provides an opportunity to reflect on the significance of the freedoms we enjoy and to commit ourselves to exercise the civic responsibilities required to sustain our constitutional system. The Constitution, including its first ten amendments, the Bill of Rights, has survived two centuries because of its unprecedented philosophical premise: that it derives its power from the people. It is not a grant from the government to the people. In 1787 the masters—the people—were saying to their government—their servant—that certain rights are inherent, natural rights and that they belong to the people, who had those rights before any governments existed. The function of government, they said, was to protect these rights.

The Bill of Rights also owes its continued vitality to the fact that it was drafted by experienced, practical politicians. It was a product of the Framers' essential mistrust of the frailties of human nature. This led them to develop the idea of the separation of powers and to make the Bill of Rights part of the permanent Constitution.

Moreover, the document was designed to be flexible, and the role of providing that flexibility through interpretation has fallen to the judiciary. Indeed, the first commander in chief, George Washington, gave the Supreme Court its moral marching orders two centuries ago when he said, "the administration of justice is the firmest pillar of government." The principle of judicial review as a check on government has perhaps nowhere been more significant than in the protection of individual liberties. It has been my privilege, along with my colleagues on the Court, to ensure the continued vitality of our Bill of Rights. As John Marshall asked, long before he became chief justice, "To what quarter will you look for a protection from an infringement on the Constitution, if you will not give the power to the judiciary?"

But the preservation of the Bill of Rights is not the sole responsibility of the judiciary. Rather, judges, legislatures, and presidents are partners with every American; liberty is the responsibility of every public officer and every citizen. In this spirit all Americans should become acquainted with the principles and history of this most remarkable document. Its bicentennial should not be simply a celebration but the beginning of an ongoing process. Americans must—by their conduct—guarantee that it continues to protect the sacred rights of our uniquely multicultural population. We must not fail to exercise our rights to vote, to participate in government and community activities, and to implement the principles of liberty, tolerance, opportunity, and justice for all.

# THE AMERICAN HERITAGE
# HISTORY OF THE BILL OF RIGHTS

### THE FIRST AMENDMENT
*by Philip A. Klinkner*

### THE SECOND AMENDMENT
*by Joan C. Hawxhurst*

### THE THIRD AMENDMENT
*by Burnham Holmes*

### THE FOURTH AMENDMENT
*by Paula A. Franklin*

### THE FIFTH AMENDMENT
*by Burnham Holmes*

### THE SIXTH AMENDMENT
*by Eden Force*

### THE SEVENTH AMENDMENT
*by Lila E. Summer*

### THE EIGHTH AMENDMENT
*by Vincent Buranelli*

### THE NINTH AMENDMENT
*by Philip A. Klinkner*

### THE TENTH AMENDMENT
*by Judith Adams*

# The Bill of Rights

## AMENDMENT 1*
**Article**   Congress shall make no law respecting an establishment of religion, or prohibiting the free exercise thereof; or abridging the freedom of speech, or of the press; or the right of the people peaceably to assemble, and to petition the Government for a redress of grievances.

## AMENDMENT 2
**Article**   A well regulated Militia, being necessary to the security of a free State, the right of the people to keep and bear Arms, shall not be infringed.

## AMENDMENT 3
**Article**   No Soldier shall, in time of peace be quartered in any house, without the consent of the Owner, nor in time of war, but in a manner to be prescribed by law.

## AMENDMENT 4
**Article**   The right of the people to be secure in their persons, houses, papers, and effects, against unreasonable searches and seizures, shall not be violated, and no Warrants shall issue, but upon probable cause, supported by Oath or affirmation, and particularly describing the place to be searched, and the persons or things to be seized.

## AMENDMENT 5
**Article**   No person shall be held to answer for a capital, or otherwise infamous crime, unless on a presentment or indictment of a Grand Jury, except in cases arising in the land or naval forces, or in the Militia, when in actual service in time of War or public danger; nor shall any person be subject for the same offence to be twice put in jeopardy of life or limb; nor shall be compelled in any criminal case to be a witness against himself, nor be deprived of life, liberty, or property, without due process of law; nor shall private property be taken for public use without just compensation.

## AMENDMENT 6
**Article**   In all criminal prosecutions, the accused shall enjoy the right to a speedy and public trial, by an impartial jury of the State and district wherein the crime shall have been committed, which district shall have been previously ascertained by law, and to be informed of the nature and cause of the accusation; to be confronted with the witnesses against him; to have compulsory process for obtaining Witnesses in his favor, and to have the assistance of counsel for his defence.

## AMENDMENT 7
**Article**   In Suits at common law, where the value in controversy shall exceed twenty dollars, the right of trial by jury shall be preserved, and no fact tried by a jury, shall be otherwise reexamined in any Court of the United States, than according to the rules of the common law.

## AMENDMENT 8
**Article**   Excessive bail shall not be required, nor excessive fines imposed, nor cruel and unusual punishments inflicted.

## AMENDMENT 9
**Article**   The enumeration in the Constitution, of certain rights, shall not be construed to deny or disparage others retained by the people.

## AMENDMENT 10
**Article**   The powers not delegated to the United States by the Constitution, nor prohibited by it to the States, are reserved to the States respectively, or to the people.

*Note that each of the first ten amendments to the original Constitution is called an "Article." None of these amendments had actual numbers at the time of their ratification.

# TIME CHART

## THE HISTORY OF THE
## BILL OF RIGHTS

### 1770s–1790s

1774 Quartering Act
1775 Revolutionary War begins
1776 Declaration of Independence is signed.
1783 Revolutionary War ends.
1787 Constitutional Convention writes the U.S. Constitution.
1788 U.S. Constitution is ratified by most states.
1789 Congress proposes the Bill of Rights
1791 The Bill of Rights is ratified by the states.
1792 Militia Act

### 1800s–1820s

1803 *Marbury* v. *Madison*. Supreme Court declares that it has the power of judicial review and exercises it. This is the first case in which the Court holds a law of Congress unconstitutional.
1807 Trial of Aaron Burr. Ruling that juries may have knowledge of a case so long as they have not yet formed an opinion.
1813 Kentucky becomes the first state to outlaw concealed weapons.
1824 *Gibbons* v. *Ogden*. Supreme Court defines Congress's power to regulate commerce, including trade between states and within states if that commerce affects other states.

## 1830s–1870s

**1833** *Barron* v. *Baltimore*. Supreme Court rules that Bill of Rights applies only to actions of the federal government, not to the states and local governments.

**1851** *Cooley* v. *Board of Wardens of the Port of Philadelphia*. Supreme Court rules that states can apply their own rules to some foreign and interstate commerce if their rules are of a local nature—unless or until Congress makes rules for particular situations.

**1857** *Dred Scott* v. *Sandford*. Supreme Court denies that African Americans are citizens even if they happen to live in a "free state."

**1862** Militia Act

**1865** Thirteenth Amendment is ratified. Slavery is not allowed in the United States.

**1868** Fourteenth Amendment is ratified. All people born or naturalized in the United States are citizens. Their privileges and immunities are protected, as are their life, liberty, and property according to due process. They have equal protection of the laws.

**1873** *Slaughterhouse* cases. Supreme Court rules that the Fourteenth Amendment does not limit state power to make laws dealing with economic matters. Court mentions the unenumerated right to political participation.

**1876** *United States* v. *Cruikshank*. Supreme Court rules that the right to bear arms for a lawful purpose is not an absolute right granted by the Constitution. States can limit this right and make their own gun-control laws.

## 1880s–1920s

**1884** *Hurtado* v. *California*. Supreme Court rules that the right to a grand jury indictment doesn't apply to the states.

**1896** *Plessy* v. *Ferguson*. Supreme Court upholds a state law based on "separate but equal" facilities for different races.

**1903** Militia Act creates National Guard.

**1905** *Lochner* v. *New York*. Supreme Court strikes down a state law regulating maximum work hours.

**1914** *Weeks* v. *United States*. Supreme Court establishes that illegally obtained evidence, obtained by unreasonable search and seizure, cannot be used in federal trials.

**1918** *Hammer* v. *Dagenhart*. Supreme Court declares unconstitutional a federal law prohibiting the shipment between states of goods made by young children.

**1923** *Meyer* v. *Nebraska*. Supreme Court rules that a law banning teaching of foreign languages or teaching in languages other than English is unconstitutional. Court says that certain areas of people's private lives are protected from government interference.

**1925** *Carroll* v. *United States*. Supreme Court allows searches of automobiles without a search warrant under some circumstances.

**1925** *Gitlow* v. *New York*. Supreme Court rules that freedom of speech and freedom of the press are protected from state actions by the Fourteenth Amendment.

## 1930s

**1931** *Near* v. *Minnesota*. Supreme Court rules that liberty of the press and of speech are safeguarded from state action.

**1931** *Stromberg* v. *California*. Supreme Court extends concept of freedom of speech to symbolic actions such as displaying a flag.

**1932** *Powell* v. *Alabama* (*First Scottsboro* case). Supreme Court rules that poor defendants have a right to an appointed lawyer when tried for crimes that may result in the death penalty.

**1934** National Firearms Act becomes the first federal law to restrict the keeping and bearing of arms.

**1935** *Norris* v. *Alabama* (*Second Scottsboro* case). Supreme Court reverses the conviction of an African American because of the long continued excluding of African Americans from jury service in the trial area.

**1937** *Palko* v. *Connecticut*. Supreme Court refuses to require states to protect people under the double jeopardy clause of the Bill of Rights. But the case leads to future application of individual rights in the Bill of Rights to the states on a case-by-case basis.

**1937** *DeJonge* v. *Oregon*. Supreme Court rules that freedom of assembly and petition are protected against state laws.

**1939** *United States* v. *Miller*. Supreme Court rules that National Firearms Act of 1934 does not violate Second Amendment.

## 1940s–1950s

**1940** *Cantwell* v. *Connecticut*. Supreme Court rules that free exercise of religion is protected against state laws.

**1943** *Barnette* v. *West Virginia State Board of Education*. Supreme Court rules that flag salute laws are unconstitutional.

**1946** *Theil* v. *Pacific Railroad*. Juries must be a cross section of the community, excluding no group based on religion, race, sex, or economic status.

**1947** *Everson* v. *Board of Education*. Supreme Court rules that government attempts to impose religious practices, the establishment of religion, is forbidden to the states.

**1948** *In re Oliver*. Supreme Court rules that defendants have a right to public trial in nonfederal trials.

**1949** *Wolf* v. *California*. Supreme Court rules that freedom from unreasonable searches and seizures also applies to states.

**1954** *Brown* v. *Board of Education of Topeka*. Supreme Court holds that segregation on the basis of race (in public education) denies equal protection of the laws.

**1958** *NAACP* v. *Alabama*. Supreme Court rules that the privacy of membership lists in an organization is part of the right to freedom of assembly and association.

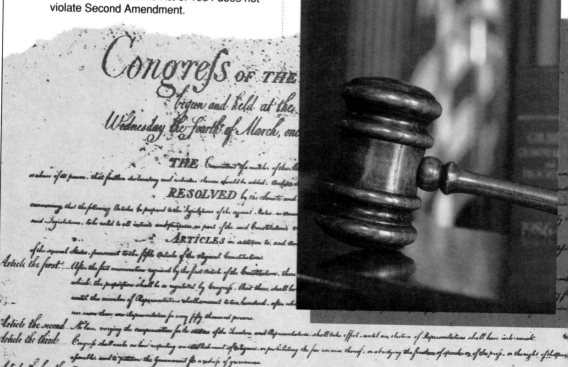

## 1960s

**1961** *Mapp* v. *Ohio.* Supreme Court rules that illegally obtained evidence must not be allowed in state criminal trials.

**1962** *Engel* v. *Vitale.* Supreme Court strikes down state-sponsored school prayer, saying it is no business of government to compose official prayers as part of a religious program carried on by the government.

**1963** *Gideon* v. *Wainwright.* Supreme Court rules that the right of people accused of serious crimes to be represented by an appointed counsel applies to state criminal trials.

**1964** Civil Rights Act is passed.

**1964** *Malloy* v. *Hogan.* Supreme Court rules that the right to protection against forced self-incrimination applies to state trials.

**1965** *Griswold* v. *Connecticut.* Supreme Court rules that there is a right to privacy in marriage and declares unconstitutional a state law banning the use of or the giving of information about birth control.

**1965** *Pointer* v. *Texas.* Supreme Court rules that the right to confront witnesses against an accused person applies to state trials.

**1966** *Parker* v. *Gladden.* Supreme Court ruling is interpreted to mean that the right to an impartial jury is applied to the states.

**1966** *Miranda* v. *Arizona.* Supreme Court extends the protection against forced self-incrimination. Police have to inform people in custody of their rights before questioning them.

**1967** *Katz* v. *United States.* Supreme Court rules that people's right to be free of unreasonable searches includes protection against electronic surveillance.

**1967** *Washington* v. *Texas.* Supreme Court rules that accused people have the right to have witnesses in their favor brought into court.

**1967** *In re Gault.* Supreme Court rules that juvenile proceedings that might lead to the young person's being sent to a state institution must follow due process and fair treatment. These include the rights against forced self-incrimination, to counsel, to confront witnesses.

**1967** *Klopfer* v. *North Carolina.* Supreme Court rules that the right to a speedy trial applies to state trials.

**1968** *Duncan* v. *Louisiana.* Supreme Court rules that the right to a jury trial in criminal cases applies to state trials.

**1969** *Benton* v. *Maryland.* Supreme Court rules that the protection against double jeopardy applies to the states.

**1969** *Brandenburg* v. *Ohio.* Supreme Court rules that speech calling for the use of force or crime can only be prohibited if it is directed to bringing about immediate lawless action and is likely to bring about such action.

## 1970s–1990s

**1970** *Williams* v. *Florida.* Juries in cases that do not lead to the possibility of the death penalty may consist of six jurors rather than twelve.

**1971** *Pentagon Papers* case. Freedom of the press is protected by forbidding prior restraint.

**1971** *Duke Power Co.* v. *Carolina Environmental Study Group, Inc.* Supreme Court upholds state law limiting liability of federally licensed power companies in the event of a nuclear accident.

**1972** *Furman* v. *Georgia.* Supreme Court rules that the death penalty (as it was then decided upon) is cruel and unusual punishment and therefore unconstitutional.

**1972** *Argersinger* v. *Hamlin.* Supreme Court rules that right to counsel applies to all criminal cases that might involve a jail term.

**1973** *Roe* v. *Wade.* Supreme Court declares that the right to privacy protects a woman's right to end pregnancy by abortion under specified circumstances.

**1976** *Gregg* v. *Georgia.* Supreme Court rules that the death penalty is to be allowed if it is decided upon in a consistent and reasonable way, if the sentencing follows strict guidelines, and if the penalty is not required for certain crimes.

**1976** *National League of Cities* v. *Usery.* Supreme Court holds that the Tenth Amendment prevents Congress from making federal minimum wage and overtime rules apply to state and city workers.

**1981** *Quilici* v. *Village of Morton Grove.* U.S. district court upholds a local ban on sale and possession of handguns.

**1985** *Garcia* v. *San Antonio Metropolitan Transit Authority.* Supreme Court rules that Congress can make laws dealing with wages and hour rules applied to city-owned transportation systems.

**1989** *Webster* v. *Reproductive Health Services.* Supreme Court holds that a state may prohibit all use of public facilities and publicly employed staff in abortions.

**1989** *Johnson* v. *Texas.* Supreme Court rules that flag burning is protected and is a form of "symbolic speech."

**1990** *Cruzan* v. *Missouri Department of Health.* Supreme Court recognizes for the first time a very sick person's right to die without being forced to undergo unwanted medical treatment and a person's right to a living will.

**1990** *Noriega–CNN* case. Supreme Court upholds lower federal court's decision to allow temporary prior restraint thus limiting the First Amendment right of freedom of the press.

# The Birth of the Bill of Rights

"We hold these truths to be self-evident, that all men are created equal, that they are endowed by their Creator with certain unalienable Rights, that among these are Life, Liberty, and the pursuit of Happiness."

THE DECLARATION OF INDEPENDENCE (1776)

A brave Chinese student standing in front of a line of tanks, Eastern Europeans marching against the secret police, happy crowds dancing on top of the Berlin Wall—these were recent scenes of people trying to gain their freedom or celebrating it. The scenes and the events that sparked them will live on in history. They also show the lasting gift that is our Bill of Rights. The freedoms guaranteed by the Bill of Rights have guided and inspired millions of people all over the world in their struggle for freedom.

## The Colonies Gain Their Freedom

Like many countries today, the United States fought to gain freedom and democracy for itself. The American colonies had a revolution from 1775 to 1783 to free themselves from British rule.

The colonists fought to free themselves because they believed that the British had violated, or gone against, their rights. The colonists held what some considered the extreme idea that all

James Madison is known as both the "Father of the Constitution" and the "Father of the Bill of Rights." In 1789 he proposed to Congress the amendments that became the Bill of Rights. Madison served two terms as president of the United States from 1809 to 1817.

*The Raising of the Liberty Pole* by John McRae. In 1776, American colonists hoisted liberty poles as symbols of liberty and freedom from British rule. At the top they usually placed a liberty cap. Such caps resembled the caps given to slaves in ancient Rome when they were freed.

persons are born with certain rights. They believed that these rights could not be taken away, even by the government. The importance our nation gave to individual rights can be seen in the Declaration of Independence. The Declaration, written by Thomas Jefferson in 1776, states:

> We hold these truths to be self-evident, that all men are created equal, that they are endowed by their Creator with certain unalienable Rights, that among these are Life, Liberty, and the pursuit of Happiness.

The United States won its independence from Britain in 1783. But with freedom came the difficult job of forming a government. The Americans wanted a government that was strong enough to keep peace and prosperity, but not so strong that it might take away the rights for which the Revolution had been fought. The Articles of Confederation was the country's first written plan of government.

The Articles of Confederation, becoming law in 1781, created a weak national government. The defects in the Articles soon became clear to many Americans. Because the United States did not have a strong national government, its economy suffered. Under the Articles, Congress did not have the power to tax. It had to ask the states for money or borrow it. There was no separate president or court system. Nine of the states had to agree before Congress's bills became law. In 1786 economic problems caused farmers in Massachusetts to revolt. The national government was almost powerless to stop the revolt. It was also unable to build an army or navy strong enough to protect the United States's borders and its ships on the high seas.

## The Constitution Is Drawn Up

The nation's problems had to be solved. So, in February 1787, the Continental Congress asked the states to send delegates to a convention to discuss ways of improving the Articles. That May, fifty-five delegates, from every state except Rhode Island, met in Philadelphia. The group included some of the country's most famous leaders: George Washington, hero of the Revolution; Benjamin Franklin, publisher, inventor, and diplomat; and James Madison, a leading critic of the Articles. Madison would soon become the guiding force behind the Constitutional Convention.

After a long, hot summer of debate the delegates finally drew up the document that became the U.S. Constitution. It set up a strong central government. But it also divided power between three branches of the federal government. These three branches were the executive branch (the presidency), the legislative branch (Congress), and the judicial branch (the courts). Each was given one part of the government's power. This division was to make sure that no single branch became so powerful that it could violate the people's rights.

The legislative branch (made up of the House of Representatives and the Senate) would have the power to pass laws, raise taxes and spend money, regulate the national economy, and declare war. The executive branch was given the power to carry out the laws, run foreign affairs, and command the military.

*The Signing of the Constitution* painted by Thomas Rossiter. The Constitutional Convention met in Philadelphia from May into September 1787. The proposed Constitution contained protection for some individual rights such as protection against *ex post facto* laws and bills of attainder. When the Constitution was ratified by the required number of states in 1788, however, it did not have a bill of rights.

The role of the judicial branch in this plan was less clear. The Constitution said that the judicial branch would have "judicial power." However, it was unclear exactly what this power was. Over the years "judicial power" has come to mean "judicial review." The power of judicial review allows the federal courts to reject laws passed by Congress or the state legislatures that they believe violate the Constitution.

Judicial review helps protect our rights. It allows federal courts to reject laws that violate the Constitution's guarantees of individual rights. Because of this power, James Madison believed that the courts would be an "impenetrable bulwark," an unbreakable wall, against any attempt by government to take away these rights.

The Constitution did more than divide the power of the federal government among the three branches. It also divided power between the states and the federal government. This division of power is known as *federalism*. Federalism means that the federal

government has control over certain areas. These include regulating the national economy and running foreign and military affairs. The states have control over most other areas. For example, they regulate their economies and make most other laws. Once again, the Framers (writers) of the Constitution hoped that the division of powers would keep both the states and the federal government from becoming too strong and possibly violating individual rights.

The new Constitution did *not,* however, contain a bill of rights. Such a bill would list the people's rights and would forbid the government from interfering with them. The only discussion of the topic came late in the convention. At that time, George Mason of Virginia called for a bill of rights. A Connecticut delegate, Roger Sherman, disagreed. He claimed that a bill of rights was not needed. In his view, the Constitution did not take away any of the rights in the bills of rights in the state constitutions. These had been put in place during the Revolution. The other delegates agreed with Roger Sherman. Mason's proposal was voted down by all.

Yet the Constitution was not without guarantees of individual rights. One of these rights was the protection of *habeas corpus.* This is a legal term that refers to the right of someone who has been arrested to be brought into court and formally charged with a crime. Another right forbade *ex post facto* laws. These are laws that outlaw actions that took place before the passage of the laws. Other parts of the Constitution forbade bills of attainder (laws pronouncing a person guilty of a crime without trial), required jury trials, restricted convictions for treason, and guaranteed a republican form of government. That is a government in which political power rests with citizens who vote for elected officials and representatives responsible to the voters. The Constitution also forbade making public officials pass any "religious test." This meant that religious requirements could not be forced on public officials.

## The Debate Over the New Constitution

Once it was written, the Constitution had to be ratified, or approved, by nine of the states before it could go into effect. The new

Constitution created much controversy. Heated battles raged in many states over whether or not to approve the document. One of the main arguments used by those who opposed the Constitution (the Anti-Federalists) was that the Constitution made the federal government too strong. They feared that it might violate the rights of the people just as the British government had. Although he had helped write the Constitution, Anti-Federalist George Mason opposed it for this reason. He claimed that he would sooner chop off his right hand than put it to the Constitution as it then stood.

To correct what they viewed as flaws in the Constitution, the Anti-Federalists insisted that it have a bill of rights. The fiery orator of the Revolution, Patrick Henry, another Anti-Federalist, exclaimed, "Liberty, the greatest of all earthly blessings—give us that precious jewel, and you may take every thing else!"

Although he was not an Anti-Federalist, Thomas Jefferson also believed that a bill of rights was needed. He wrote a letter to James Madison, a wavering Federalist, in which he said: "A bill of rights is what the people are entitled to against every government on earth."

Supporters of the Constitution (the Federalists) argued that it did not need a bill of rights. One reason they stated, similar to that given at the Philadelphia convention, was that most state constitutions had a bill of rights. Nothing in the Constitution would limit or abolish these rights. In 1788 James Madison wrote that he thought a bill of rights would provide only weak "parchment barriers" against attempts by government to take away individual rights. He believed that history had shown that a bill of rights was ineffective on "those occasions when its control [was] needed most."

The views of the Anti-Federalists seem to have had more support than did those of the Federalists. The Federalists came to realize that without a bill of rights, the states might not approve the new Constitution. To ensure ratification, the Federalists therefore agreed to support adding a bill of rights to the Constitution.

With this compromise, eleven of the thirteen states ratified the Constitution by July 1788. The new government of the United States was born. The two remaining states, North Carolina and

Rhode Island, in time accepted the new Constitution. North Carolina approved it in November 1789 and Rhode Island in May 1790.

## James Madison Calls for a Bill of Rights

On April 30, 1789, George Washington took the oath of office as president. The new government was launched. One of its first jobs was to amend, or change, the Constitution to include a bill of rights. This is what many of the states had called for during the ratification process. Leading this effort in the new Congress was James Madison. He was a strong supporter of individual rights. As a member of the Virginia legislature, he had helped frame the Virginia Declaration of Rights. He had also fought for religious liberty.

Madison, however, had at first opposed including a bill of rights. But his views had changed. He feared that the Constitution would not be ratified by enough states to become law unless the Federalists offered to include a bill of rights. Madison also knew that many people were afraid of the new government. He feared they might oppose its actions or attempt to undo it. He said a bill of rights "will kill the opposition everywhere, and by putting an end to disaffection to [discontent with] the Government itself, enable the administration to venture on measures not otherwise safe."

On June 8, 1789, the thirty-eight-year-old Madison rose to speak in the House of Representatives. He called for several changes to the Constitution that contained the basis of our present Bill of Rights. Despite his powerful words, Madison's speech did not excite his listeners. Most Federalists in Congress opposed a bill of rights. Others believed that the new Constitution should be given more time to operate before Congress considered making any changes. Many Anti-Federalists wanted a new constitutional convention. There, they hoped to greatly limit the powers of the federal government. These Anti-Federalists thought that adding a bill of rights to the Constitution would prevent their movement for a new convention.

Finally, in August, Madison persuaded the House to consider

his amendments. The House accepted most of them. However, instead of being placed in the relevant sections of the Constitution, as Madison had called for, the House voted to add them as separate amendments. This change—listing the amendments together—made the Bill of Rights the distinct document that it is today.

After approval by the House, the amendments went to the Senate. The Senate dropped what Madison considered the most important part of his plan. This was the protection of freedom of the press, freedom of religious belief, and the right to trial by jury from violation by the states. Protection of these rights from violation by state governments would have to wait until after the Fourteenth Amendment was adopted in 1868.

The House and the Senate at last agreed on ten amendments to protect individual rights. What rights were protected? Here is a partial list:

The First Amendment protects freedom of religion, of speech, of the press, of peaceful assembly, and of petition.

The Second Amendment gives to the states the right to keep a militia (a volunteer, reserve military force) and to the people the right to keep and bear arms.

The Third Amendment prevents the government from keeping troops in private homes during wartime.

The Fourth Amendment protects individuals from unreasonable searches and seizures by the government.

The Fifth Amendment states that the government must get an indictment (an official ruling that a crime has been committed) before someone can be tried for a serious crime. This amendment bans "double jeopardy." This means trying a person twice for the same criminal offense. It also protects people from having to testify against themselves in court.

The Fifth Amendment also says that the government cannot take away a person's "life, liberty, or property, without due process of law." This means that the government must follow fair and just procedures if it takes away a person's "life, liberty, or property." Finally, the Fifth Amendment says that if the government takes property from an individual for public use, it must pay that person an adequate sum of money for the property.

The Sixth Amendment requires that all criminal trials be speedy and public, and decided by a fair jury. The amendment also allows people on trial to know what offense they have been charged with. It also allows them to be present when others testify against them, to call witnesses to their defense, and to have the help of a lawyer.

The Seventh Amendment provides for a jury trial in all cases involving amounts over $20.

The Eighth Amendment forbids unreasonably high bail (money paid to free someone from jail before his or her trial), unreasonably large fines, and cruel and unusual punishments.

The Ninth Amendment says that the rights of the people are not limited only to those listed in the Bill of Rights.

Finally, the Tenth Amendment helps to establish federalism by giving to the states and the people any powers not given to the federal government by the Constitution.

After being approved by the House and the Senate, the amendments were sent to the states for adoption in October 1789. By December 1791, three-fourths of the states had approved the ten amendments we now know as the Bill of Rights. The Bill of Rights had become part of the U.S. Constitution.


## How Our Court System Works

Many of the events in this book concern court cases involving the Bill of Rights. To help understand how the U.S. court system works, here is a brief description.

The U.S. federal court system has three levels. At the lowest level are the federal district courts. There are ninety-four district courts, each covering a different area of the United States and its territories. Most cases having to do with the Constitution begin in the district courts.

People who lose their cases in the district courts may then appeal to the next level in the court system, the federal courts of appeals. To appeal means to take your case to a higher court in an attempt to change the lower court's decision. Here, those who are making the appeal try to obtain a different judgment. There are thirteen federal courts of appeals in the United States.

People who lose in the federal courts of appeals may then take their case to the U.S. Supreme Court. It is the highest court in the land. The Supreme Court has the final say in a case. You cannot appeal a Supreme Court decision.

The size of the Supreme Court is set by Congress and has changed over the years. Since 1869 the Supreme Court has been made up of nine justices. One is the chief justice of the United States, and eight are associate justices. The justices are named by the president and confirmed by the Senate.

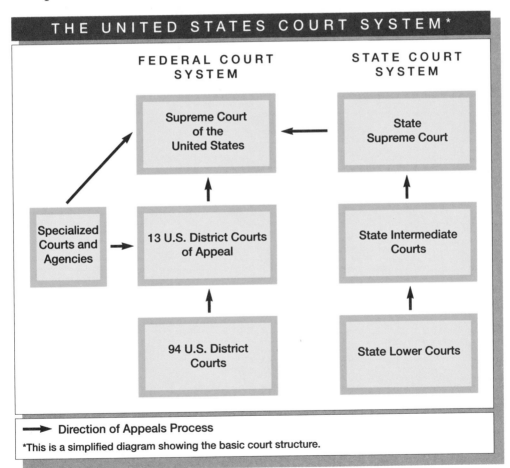

**THE UNITED STATES COURT SYSTEM***

FEDERAL COURT SYSTEM

STATE COURT SYSTEM

Supreme Court of the United States

State Supreme Court

Specialized Courts and Agencies

13 U.S. District Courts of Appeal

State Intermediate Courts

94 U.S. District Courts

State Lower Courts

➤ Direction of Appeals Process

*This is a simplified diagram showing the basic court structure.

In the Supreme Court, a simple majority of votes is needed to decide a case. If there is a tie, the lower court's decision remains in effect. When the chief justice votes on the majority side, he or she can assign the writing of the opinion to any of the majority justices, including himself or herself. The opinion states the Court's decision and the reasons for it. Who writes the opinion when the chief justice hasn't voted on the majority side? In that case, the longest-serving associate justice who voted for the majority decision can assign the writing to any of the majority justices, including himself or herself.

What if a justice has voted for the majority decision but doesn't agree with the reasons given in the majority opinion? He or she may write what is called a concurring opinion. That is one which agrees with the Court's decision but for different reasons.

Those justices who disagree with the Court's decision may write what is called a dissenting opinion. They have the opportunity to explain why they think the majority Supreme Court decision is wrong.

In addition to the federal court system, each state has its own system of courts. These systems vary from state to state. However, they are usually made up of two or three levels of lower courts and then the state's highest court, usually called the state supreme court. Those who lose their cases in the state supreme court may appeal those decisions to the federal court system, usually to the Supreme Court.

Not all cases that are appealed to the Supreme Court are heard by it. In fact, very few of them are. For the Supreme Court to decide to hear a case, four of the nine justices must vote to hear it. If fewer than four justices vote to hear the case, then the judgment of the lower court remains in effect.

## The Importance of the Fifth Amendment

Without a doubt, the Fifth Amendment ranks as one of the most crucial amendments in the entire Constitution of the United States.

With beginnings reaching as far back as thirteenth-century England, this amendment covers a wide range of safeguards. From the grand jury system to the protection against double jeopardy, from the power of eminent domain to the right against self-incrimination and the all-important due process of law—how different the history of the United States would have been without the Fifth Amendment.

Long ago the Fifth Amendment became a set of rights that all too often we take for granted. As the history of the Fifth Amendment unfolds in the following chapters, you might pause from time to time to think about what life in the United States would be like today without the safeguards of this amendment.

PHILIP A. KLINKNER

# An Overview of the Fifth Amendment

"No person shall be held to answer for a capital, or otherwise infamous crime, unless on a presentment or indictment of a Grand Jury, except in cases arising in the land or naval forces, or in the Militia, when in actual service in time of War or public danger; nor shall any person be subject for the same offence to be twice put in jeopardy of life or limb; nor shall be compelled in any criminal case to be a witness against himself, nor be deprived of life, liberty, or property, without due process of law; nor shall private property be taken for public use, without just compensation." THE FIFTH AMENDMENT

**W**hy should anyone today read about the history and importance of the Fifth Amendment?

"Historic continuity with the past is not a duty," wrote Justice Oliver Wendell Holmes in 1920, "it is only a necessity."

In other words, we do not really know the importance of an issue in the present until we get our bearings by studying the past. It is not unlike the sailors of ancient times. They plotted their way across unknown seas by studying the position of the stars. By studying the amendments that are like the stars in our constitutional "heavens," we are able to understand the difficult legal issues of the present. We are able to make the decisions that will affect the unknown that lies ahead.

## Alexander Hamilton and the Bill of Rights

Alexander Hamilton, the brilliant representative from New York at the 1787 Constitutional Convention, favored a strong national

Alexander Hamilton attended the Constitutional Convention of 1787 and was a supporter of a strong national government. He served as U.S. secretary of the treasury from 1789 to 1795. Hamilton was a leading Federalist who opposed attaching a bill of rights to the U.S. Constitution.

government. In a series of essays published in 1788 in *The Federalist* (written with John Jay and James Madison), Hamilton discussed why it was not necessary to have a bill of rights.

"I go further, and affirm that bills of rights . . . are not only unnecessary in the proposed Constitution, but would even be dangerous. They would contain various exceptions to powers not granted. . . ." Hamilton's position, given his argument, was as follows: Congress does not have the power, for example, to limit free speech. So why should there be a bill of rights to forbid it from limiting free speech?

Hamilton was only half right. He was wrong that the Bill of Rights was unnecessary. This document has remained one of the major strengths of American democracy. For no matter who is running the government or what is going on in the world, this now-faded parchment remains a constant ray of hope to those who fight for and preserve democracy.

## The Grand Jury

The right to a grand jury is the first right covered in the Fifth Amendment. The grand jury at the federal level is made up of sixteen to twenty-three citizens and at the state level is made up of twelve to twenty-three citizens. It is larger than the petit, or small, jury of six to twelve citizens used to determine the outcome of trials tried in a courtroom. That is why it has the name grand jury.

The grand jury was set up to weigh the evidence in order to find out if there is a need to have a trial. If there is "probable cause," that is, a likelihood that the charges are true, the grand jury votes that a trial be held. If there is not enough evidence, the grand jury votes that the case *not* go to trial. The purpose of the grand jury is to keep people from having to undergo the ordeal of an uncalled-for trial.

"Historically, this body [the grand jury]," said Earl Warren, the chief justice of the United States from 1953 to 1969, "has been regarded as a primary security to the innocent against hasty, malicious and oppressive persecution."

## The Military Courts

The next rights covered in the Fifth Amendment apply to the system of military courts. People who serve in the U.S. armed forces and in the militia are judged by a set of standards and rules made especially for military courts. These courts are very different from the courts for civilians. The rule book that spells out the military system of justice is known as the Uniform Code of Military Justice. It was written by Congress and presented to the armed services in 1950.

When he was the newest associate justice on the Supreme Court, William H. Rehnquist stated the view in the case of *Parker* v. *Levy* (1974) that within the military system people do not have the same legal protections as civilians do. The case dealt with a doctor, a captain in the army, who acted with "conduct unbecoming an officer and a gentleman." The Third Circuit Court said that this phrase was unnecessarily vague and violated the due process clause of the Fifth Amendment. Justice William H. Rehnquist wrote: "The fundamental necessity for obedience, and the consequent necessity for imposition of discipline, may render permissible within the military that which would be constitutionally impermissible outside it."

Justice William H. Rehnquist also had this to say about the role of the military. "This Court has long recognized that the military is, by necessity, a specialized society separate from civilian society. We have also recognized that the military has, again by necessity, developed laws and traditions of its own during its long history."

Throughout this book, the legal citation of a decided court case is shown in the following standard way: the names of the parties in the legal case and the year of the decision. The first name is the

U.S. Marines in training. According to the Fifth Amendment, the rules regarding grand juries do not hold true for members of the armed forces in times of war or danger to the country.

party that appealed or took the case to a higher court. The "v." stands for versus, which means "against." The second name is the party that responded or answered. For example, Parker is the party who brought the case to the Court, and Levy responded. In U.S.

Supreme Court cases—the only court cases that appear in this book with the exception of one case from the Military Court of Appeals—the second name is the name of the successful party in a case tried before a lower court. The first name is the name of the loser who is appealing from the lower court.

## The Right Against Double Jeopardy

The next Fifth Amendment right deals with double jeopardy. Double jeopardy means being tried twice for the same crime. The prevention of double jeopardy is one of the oldest safeguards in Western civilization.

In colonial Massachusetts, double jeopardy was forbidden by the Massachusetts Body of Liberties of 1641: "No man shall be twice sentenced by civil justice for one and the same crime, offense, or trespass."

Over 300 years later, in 1957, Justice Hugo L. Black of the U.S. Supreme Court stated the need for this protection. "The State with all its resources and power should not be allowed to make repeated attempts to convict an individual."

## The Right Against Self-Incrimination

This is the right that many people think of when they hear the Fifth Amendment mentioned. Self-incrimination includes acts or statements at or before a trial by which a person provides possible evidence involving himself or herself in a crime. The right against forced self-incrimination is also one of the most important rights guaranteed in the Bill of Rights.

Beginning with religious courts in the thirteenth and fourteenth centuries and then political courts starting in the fifteenth century, witnesses were required to take an oath. This was the dreaded *ex officio* ("by virtue of an office") oath. This means that the questioner has the authority, because of his office, to demand answers. How it worked was as follows. The witness was sworn to

A witness being questioned. The due process clause of the Fifth Amendment has been interpreted to require that the legal processes developed over many years are fair. The government is supposed to act fairly in all it does in applying the laws.

tell the truth. The questioner was free to ask any number of questions and to take any line of questioning. The person being examined would most likely not know the details of the matter under investigation. Needless to say, he or she had no idea what the answers might later be used to prove.

As Justice William O. Douglas declared: "[T]he Fifth Amendment was written in part to prevent any Congress, any court, and any prosecutor from prying open the lips of an accused [person] to make incriminating statements against his will.''

## The Importance of Due Process

The next right in the Fifth Amendment is that covered in the clause ''nor be deprived of life, liberty, or property, without due process of law.'' The right of the people to due process of law began with Magna Carta. King John of England signed this document in 1215 to calm angry nobles who were just about ready to take up arms. This document guaranteed what became equated in later years with the people's right to due process of law. And this right of English law became an important source for James Madison, not only in writing the Fifth Amendment, but also in writing the entire Bill of Rights.

## What Is Due Process?

The people's right to due process of law is at the very heart of the U.S. Constitution. Developed over the years, due process is a set of procedures that is followed according to established rules and principles. Due process is closely related to *stare decisis*. This is a Latin term meaning ''let the decision stand'' or ''to rule by decided matters.'' *Stare decisis* is the policy of following the rules or precedents set down in the decisions in earlier judicial cases. In other words, what is at issue in a case will be interpreted in light of an earlier case or cases.

Due process is the legal process guaranteed under both the Fifth and Fourteenth Amendments to protect citizens from the government's stepping in and unlawfully taking away life, liberty, or property. Due process of law is what shields the individual from being crushed by the state.

Down through the years, due process of law has become one of the most important concepts in the U.S. Constitution. So important is it that it is now separated into procedural due process of law, both civil and criminal, and substantive due process of law.

## Procedural Due Process of Law

Procedural due process of law is the guarantee that the legal processes that have been developed over many years are fair. Procedural due process means that government, in all that it does, must act fairly in applying the laws.

A good example of procedural due process is the series of steps that are followed in a court case, especially the jury trial. There is the selection and swearing in of the jury, the prosecution's case against the defendant, the defense's case, the questioning of witnesses, the judge's instructions to the jury, the jury's verdict. "It is basically the community's assurance," observed political scientist David Fellman, "that prosecutors, judges and juries will behave properly, within rules distilled [boiled down] from long centuries of concrete experience."

## Substantive Due Process of Law

Whereas procedural due process has to do with *how* government administers the laws, substantive due process involves the content of the law itself. Substantive due process asks the question: Are the laws fair to begin with?

The meaning of substantive due process of law was spelled out in 1881 by Justice Oliver Wendell Holmes, Jr. "The life of the law has not been logic; it has been experience," wrote Holmes in Lecture I of *The Common Law.* " . . . The law embodies [contains] the story of a nation's development through many centuries, and it cannot be dealt with as if it contained only the axioms [fundamental laws] and corollaries [conclusions from the facts] of a book of mathematics. In order to know what it is, we must know what it has been and what it tends to become."

## Eminent Domain

Eminent domain is a strange-sounding term that stands for the group of ideas in the closing words of the Fifth Amendment. The clause on eminent domain states: "nor shall private property be taken for public use, without just compensation."

Eminent domain deals with the power of government to take private property for a public use. Thomas I. Wharton stated this in formal terms. He wrote: "The right of eminent domain, or inherent sovereign power, gives the Legislature the control of private property for public use."

But does the property owner lose out when the government takes his or her property? No, the owner must be given "just compensation" (a reasonable amount of money) for this loss.

Of course, money may not always be enough. There are times when a house or property has great inner value for the owner. For instance, a person may have always lived in the same house and would not think of selling it for any price. In such a case, any amount of money might seem unjust.

## A Last Look

Alexander Hamilton believed that a bill of rights would grow to include more than was originally pictured by the Framers of the Constitution. This expansion is particularly true of the Fifth Amendment. But that is the strength of the Fifth Amendment. Instead of restricting the U.S. Constitution and limiting the American people, it grows and changes to meet the demands of our complex, modern life.

# Congrefs of the United States

### begun and held at the City of New-York, on
### Wednesday the fourth of March, one thousand seven hundred and eighty nine.

**THE** Conventions of a number of the States, having at the time of their adopting the Constitution, expressed a desire, in order to prevent misconstruction or abuse of its powers, that further declaratory and restrictive clauses should be added: And as extending the ground of public confidence in the Government, will best ensure the beneficent ends of its institution.

**RESOLVED** by the Senate and House of Representatives of the United States of America, in Congress assembled, two thirds of both Houses concurring, that the following Articles be proposed to the Legislatures of the several States, as amendments to the Constitution of the United States, all, or any of which Articles, when ratified by three fourths of the said Legislatures, to be valid to all intents and purposes, as part of the said Constitution; viz.

**ARTICLES** in addition to, and Amendment of the Constitution of the United States of America, proposed by Congress, and ratified by the Legislatures of the several States, pursuant to the fifth Article of the original Constitution.

**Article the first.** After the first enumeration required by the first Article of the Constitution, there shall be one Representative for every thirty thousand, until the number shall amount to one hundred, after which the proportion shall be so regulated by Congress, that there shall be not less than one hundred Representatives, nor less than one Representative for every forty thousand persons, until the number of Representatives shall amount to two hundred; after which the proportion shall be so regulated by Congress, that there shall not be less than two hundred Representatives, nor more than one Representative for every fifty thousand persons.

**Article the second.** No law, varying the compensation for the services of the Senators and Representatives, shall take effect, until an election of Representatives shall have intervened.

**Article the third.** Congress shall make no law respecting an establishment of religion, or prohibiting the free exercise thereof; or abridging the freedom of speech, or of the press; or the right of the people peaceably to assemble, and to petition the Government for a redress of grievances.

**Article the fourth.** A well regulated militia, being necessary to the security of a free State, the right of the people to keep and bear Arms, shall not be infringed.

**Article the fifth.** No Soldier shall, in time of peace be quartered in any house, without the consent of the owner, nor in time of war, but in a manner to be prescribed by law.

**Article the sixth.** The right of the people to be secure in their persons, houses, papers, and effects, against unreasonable searches and seizures, shall not be violated, and no Warrants shall issue, but upon probable cause, supported by oath or affirmation, and particularly describing the place to be searched, and the persons or things to be seized.

**Article the seventh.** No person shall be held to answer for a capital, or otherwise infamous crime, unless on a presentment or indictment of a Grand Jury, except in cases arising in the land or naval forces, or in the Militia, when in actual service in time of War or public danger; nor shall any person be subject for the same offence to be twice put in jeopardy of life or limb; nor shall be compelled in any criminal case to be a witness against himself, nor be deprived of life, liberty, or property, without due process of law; nor shall private property be taken for public use, without just compensation.

**Article the eighth.** In all criminal prosecutions, the accused shall enjoy the right to a speedy and public trial, by an impartial jury of the State and district wherein the crime shall have been committed, which district shall have been previously ascertained by law, and to be informed of the nature and cause of the accusation; to be confronted with the witnesses against him; to have compulsory process for obtaining witnesses in his favor, and to have the assistance of Counsel for his defence.

**Article the ninth.** In suits at common law, where the value in controversy shall exceed twenty dollars, the right of trial by jury shall be preserved, and no fact tried by a jury, shall be otherwise re-examined in any court of the United States, than according to the rules of the common law.

**Article the tenth.** Excessive bail shall not be required, nor excessive fines imposed, nor cruel and unusual punishments inflicted.

**Article the eleventh.** The enumeration in the Constitution, of certain rights, shall not be construed to deny or disparage others retained by the people.

**Article the twelfth.** The powers not delegated to the United States by the Constitution, nor prohibited by it to the States, are reserved to the States respectively, or to the people.

**ATTEST,**

Frederick Augustus Muhlenberg, Speaker of the House of Representatives.

John Adams, Vice President of the United States, and President of the Senate.

John Beckley, Clerk of the House of Representatives.

Sam. A. Otis, Secretary of the Senate.

# The Grand Jury:
# Listening to the Evidence

"No person shall be held to answer for a capital, or otherwise infamous crime, unless on a presentment or indictment of a Grand Jury, except in cases arising in the land or naval forces, or in the Militia, when in actual service in time of War or public danger. . . . "

THE FIFTH AMENDMENT, 1791

Take a closer look at what this opening passage of the Fifth Amendment means. It has quite a bit of technical language. But once the terms are defined the meaning will become clear. A capital crime is one that can be punishable by death. An infamous crime is a serious crime punishable by more than one year in prison. A presentment is a written accusation of criminal wrongdoing prepared, signed, and presented to the prosecutor by members of the grand jury. An indictment, on the other hand, is a formal accusation prepared by the prosecutor and agreed to by the grand jury. It states that there is probable cause that someone has committed a crime. A grand jury is the group of 12 to 23 people who listen to the evidence presented. Thus, this first part of the Fifth Amendment means that a person must be accused by a grand jury before being put on trial for a crime that can be punished by death or for any other serious crime punishable by at least a year in prison.

---

In 1789 Congress proposed twelve articles of amendment to the Constitution. Except for the first two, they were ratified by the required number of states by December 15, 1791. The seventh article of the original proposal became the Fifth Amendment.

There is no grand jury for people on active duty in the military forces. Persons in the armed forces or militia fall under a system of courts-martial (military courts) covered by the rules of military justice. For people in the military forces, crimes that are not "service connected" may be tried in civil courts. (For a fuller discussion of these issues, see Chapter 3.)

The significance of the grand jury was summarized in the decision in the case of *Wood* v. *Georgia* (1962): "[The grand jury] serves the . . . function in our society of standing between accuser and accused, . . . to determine whether a charge is founded upon reason or was dictated by an intimidating power or by malice and personal ill will."

## You and the Grand Jury

Imagine you have been called to serve on a grand jury. As foreman or forewoman (chairperson and spokesperson) of the grand jury, you look down at the piece of paper in your hand. The time has come for you and your fellow members of the grand jury to announce your decision. What have you written on the indictment (formal accusation)? Will you read out "A TRUE BILL" or "NO TRUE BILL"? Your decision depends upon whether you and the other grand jurors have voted that the evidence presented by the prosecutor *shows* or *does not show* probable cause that a crime has been committed.

But this is the end result of a modern-day grand jury. To understand how the present grand jury system works, we need to take a look back at its beginnings.

## The Beginnings of the Grand Jury System

In the year 1166, King Henry II of England started the use of the inquest, which is an official investigation. According to a law known as the Grand Assize (session) of Clarendon, the procedure

Henry II, king of England from 1154 to 1189. Under his rule, there were judicial reforms in England, including the procedure known as the inquest.

was to place a group of neighbors under oath. There were sixteen men all together. Four came from the village where the crime or dispute took place. Twelve came from the hundred in which the village was located. (A hundred was a district smaller than a county. Originally, it was probably the amount of land needed to support a hundred families.) These men were then questioned by the king's officials about a person under suspicion. The problem may have been a land dispute. Or the person may have been thought to have committed a crime. If there was enough evidence against the person, the findings of the inquest were handed over to a judge. The judge would then decide the case.

This forerunner of the grand jury system was used to capture the king's enemies. However, over the years the grand jury changed. Eventually it came to be called a presenting jury. The purpose was to find out whether there was enough evidence to hold a trial. If there was enough evidence, those findings were sent to the next stage. The presenting jury served as a safeguard, a protective hearing for the common person.

## Old Ways in the New Country

When English settlers arrived in America, they brought with them this tradition of a protective hearing for the common person against the rule of the Crown. In the English colonies it first became law in 1683 in New York's Charter of Liberties and Privileges. This charter (group of rules and laws) declared in part: "That in all Cases Capitall or Criminall there shall be a grand Inquest who shall first present the offence." This safeguard is echoed in the words that James Madison wrote more than a hundred years later in the opening passage of the Fifth Amendment.

## The Grand Jury in Action

What happens during a grand jury hearing? Today, citizens are called together to hear an indictment, or formal accusation, presented by a district attorney or another prosecutor. An indictment is the written accusation naming the person charged with a crime and charging the person with the crime. From time to time, a judge assists and advises jurors. The judge is not present all the time. The activities of the grand jury are carried out in secret. No reporters or other news media are allowed in the grand jury room.

Grand jurors are able to subpoena, or summon, witnesses. They can also ask to see almost any type of evidence. They can even request evidence that would not be allowed during a trial.

The witnesses called to testify are placed under oath and told of their right to keep silent. They are asked questions by a prosecutor or district attorney—the person trying to bring the suspect to trial. They also may be shown exhibits to refresh their memories.

Although it is part of the judicial system, the grand jury hearing is not run the way a traditional court case is run. It is all one-sided. There is no defense for the person suspected of committing a crime. Witnesses are not even allowed to have lawyers representing them in the grand jury room.

This places an extra burden on the witness, a burden that does not exist during a regular trial. The witness needs to be aware of the importance of his or her answers to every question. Any conflicting statements could possibly lead to a later perjury trial for the witness. It is not necessary to warn witnesses about the ever-present danger of perjury, or telling falsehoods, however, for witnesses are sworn to tell the truth.

Witnesses are not allowed to have lawyers inside the grand jury room. But witnesses are allowed to talk with them outside in the hall. This sometimes results in witnesses leaving the grand jury room time and again to talk with their lawyers.

Sometimes, a witness may be asked to testify in exchange for immunity, or protection from prosecution. The statements of an immunized witness can help shed light on the activities of a co-worker or superior. But what happens if someone who receives a subpoena to appear before a grand jury refuses to testify? A refusal can lead to a judgment of contempt of court. Such an offense is punishable by law.

After hearing the witnesses and looking at the evidence, the grand jurors vote on the indictment. If more than half of the grand jurors find there is probable cause to believe that a crime has been committed, then they vote ''a true bill.'' That means they vote for the indictment, which is the written accusation naming the person charged with a crime and charging the person with the crime. The case is recommended to go to trial. If more than half of the grand jurors find there is no probable cause, then they vote "no true bill." The case is not recommended to go to trial.

The grand jurors do not have to do the bidding of the prosecutor—the person trying to bring a suspect to trial. The grand jury can return a finding of "no true bill." Grand jurors also have the right to issue their own accusation of wrongdoing. This is called a presentment. (The tradition of the presentment in English and American law goes all the way back to the origin of the grand jury. It began when a group of neighbors accused a person they knew of wrongdoing.) This written accusation from the grand jury makes it necessary for the prosecutor to issue an indictment. If the prosecutor has not requested an indictment, even if he or she is reluctant to do so, the prosecutor still must issue an indictment.

## The Issue of Secrecy

The purpose of the secrecy of the grand jury hearing is to protect the different persons involved: the accused person, the names of all the people discussed during the investigation, the witnesses, and the grand jurors themselves.

It is important to remember that during a grand jury hearing, the accused person is *not* on trial. In fact, the whole purpose of the hearing is to find out if the evidence is sufficient, and the cause is probable, for the case to go to trial.

Many people may be discussed during a grand jury investigation. Their involvement could range from nothing to everything. Whatever their degree of involvement, however, people's lives could be damaged if their role became public knowledge. For the witnesses, it could be dangerous for them to return to their town or city if what they had said to the grand jury were to become common knowledge. The secrecy of the grand jury proceedings protects them.

The grand jury members work in an informal setting and are able to speak openly with each other. Suppose the jurors were to believe that what they had said would be made public. Then the effective operation of the grand jury would surely come to a halt. The grand jurors have to take an oath not to discuss the hearing outside of the room.

## When Is a Suspect Arrested?

In federal cases the indictment usually comes first. Then the suspect is arrested. At the state level, however, the grand jury indictment usually comes *after* a suspect's arrest. It may come as a surprise to learn that fewer than half of the states still use grand juries. Moreover, England gave up the grand jury system altogether in 1933.

## The Preliminary Hearing

Since most states in the United States do not use the grand jury system, they use another legal procedure—the preliminary hearing—to sift through evidence.

In a preliminary hearing, a lawyer will represent the suspect and have the right to cross-examine witnesses called by the district attorney. A judge or magistrate will decide if the evidence shows there is probable cause that a crime was committed. If there is, then instead of an indictment, a criminal information is issued. An information is a written accusation presented not by a grand jury but by a public prosecutor, charging a person with a crime.

## The Privacy Issue

One of the main purposes of the grand jury is to protect the citizen against the ordeal of an unnecessary trial. But regardless of how an investigation is done—grand jury or preliminary hearing—it can result in some sort of an invasion of a person's privacy. This is only

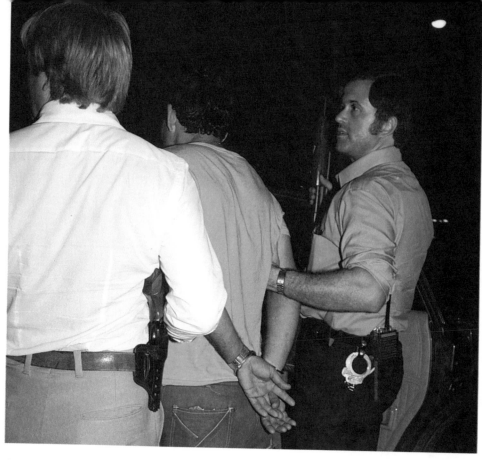

At the state level, the grand jury indictment usually occurs after the suspect has been arrested. In the many states where there is no grand jury system, the public prosecutor will issue a written criminal information charging the suspect with the crime.

made worse if there are any unofficial disclosures, or "leaks," to the public about what has gone on behind closed doors. Sometimes, leaks are enough to ruin a person's reputation or end a person's career. These disclosures can also make it far more difficult for the suspect to receive a fair trial later.

## Some Problems with the Grand Jury System

Many times, grand juries tend to do what prosecutors lead them into doing. Thus, district attorneys can sometimes turn the grand jury system into a tool of the government. Or a district attorney might be overly eager in an attempt to make a name for himself or herself. Or a prosecutor could be going out of his or her way to see that a certain person's case will go to trial.

As you might imagine, the methods used during a grand jury hearing are very different from the methods usually used in a courtroom during a trial. In a grand jury hearing, there is no give-and-take between opposing lawyers as they represent their clients. There is no impartial judge ruling on matters such as what evidence is permissible and what is impermissible.

There is no cross-examination of witnesses. (On direct examination, the lawyer often asks his or her client open-ended questions that will encourage narrative answers. An example of this would be a client's lawyer asking: "Would you describe what you do at the Widget Company?" On cross-examination, the opposing lawyer often tries to ask leading questions that will throw a witness's previous testimony into doubt and help his or her client's case. An example of this would be a lawyer asking a witness: "Why did you find it necessary to lie about your job experience in your résumé before your interview at the Widget Company?")

In fact, in a grand jury investigation, a suspect is not even able to present evidence in his or her own defense. Nevertheless, if there exists the possibility that a witness who appears before a grand jury might be prosecuted, he or she does have the right to remain silent. This right against self-incrimination is provided by a later clause in the Fifth Amendment. (For a fuller discussion of the people's right against self-incrimination, see Chapters 5 and 6.)

The grand jury may well be on the way to becoming an institution of the past. Some people say that its days of usefulness as a protection against uncontrolled authority may soon be over. They point out how the district attorney is able to control the proceedings: whom to investigate, what evidence to present, and what evidence to withhold. On the other hand, there are those who argue that it still serves a useful function. It protects the innocent as well as lends weight to the prosecution when the case does go to trial. Nevertheless, no matter which side wins out, there is no getting around the importance of the grand jury.

milton delin.       Goldar sculp.

# CHAPTER 3

# The Exception to the Grand Jury System: Military Courts

"... except in cases arising in the land or naval forces, or in the Militia, when in actual service in time of War or public danger..."

THE FIFTH AMENDMENT

**P**eople who had to go to war to win their freedom were well aware of a country's need for armed forces. So it was with the Americans as they looked back on their recent break with England. It had been only a few years earlier—on October 19, 1781—that the British had surrendered at Yorktown, Virginia. James Madison, who had graduated from Princeton University four years before the start of the Revolution in 1775, had these words to say about the importance of an army. "An efficient militia is authorized and contemplated [thought of] by the Constitution and required by the spirit of free government."

The Framers of the U.S. Constitution, however, were wary of a large standing army. They did not want the army and navy ever to become a threat to the peace and security of the government. They also wanted to be sure of keeping civilian control over the country's armed forces. They had good reason to. One of the abuses of power by King George III as noted in the Declaration of Independence had

---

Major John André was a British soldier who had been involved in a plot with Benedict Arnold to betray West Point to the British during the American Revolution. He was captured and hanged as a spy. His 1780 trial was used as a precedent for a 1940s trial.

been to make "the Military independent of and superior to the Civil power." That was why there were certain rules about the armed forces and militia in the Constitution. One was that "no Appropriation of Money to that Use shall be for a longer Term than two Years." This meant that money for the military would not be indefinite. The people's elected representatives in Congress would vote at least every two years on how much money the armed forces would get. Another was that "the President shall be Commander in Chief of the Army and Navy of the United States, and of the Militia of the several States." In other words, a civilian would be in charge of the generals.

## The Military Court System

People who serve in the army, the navy, the marines, or the air force of the United States fall under the jurisdiction, or rule, of the military court system. This was spelled out in the Constitution in Article I, Section 8: "The Congress shall have Power... To provide for... disciplining... the Militia."

In many ways, the military court system is similar to the civilian court system. However, "military law... is a jurisprudence which exists separate and apart from the law which governs in our federal judicial establishment," wrote Chief Justice Fred M. Vinson. "The Framers expressly entrusted [gave] that task to Congress."

The law book of the military is called the Uniform Code of Military Justice. It is also known as the UCMJ. The UCMJ was updated by the Military Justice Act of 1968 and that of 1983.

The Fifth Amendment is incorporated into the UCMJ. For example, military justice recognizes the importance of double jeopardy. That is, it is not permissible for a soldier or sailor to be tried twice for the same offense. The UCMJ also guarantees the soldier or sailor's right against self-incrimination. It is not allowable to force a marine or member of the air force to confess.

It is important to note, however, that there are two basic differences between the UCMJ and the Bill of Rights. One is that the UCMJ makes no provision for bail—the security for the temporary release of a prisoner before trial. The other basic difference from civil law is that in military law there is no jury trial. (There is also no grand jury.) Instead of a jury, there is either a panel of military people named by the commanding officer or there is a judge. The defendant has the option of choosing which one will hand down a verdict in the case. The defendant is not free, of course, to choose what type of court-martial he or she will face.

## Types of Courts-Martial

For the most serious offenses, such as murder, mutiny, and spying, there is the general court-martial. A military judge is in charge of this court. The panel has at least five military members. And there must be a lawyer for each side.

For any offense, except those punishable by death, there is the special court-martial. This court includes at least three members, one of whom is the presiding officer. If the trial counsel is a lawyer in the special court-martial, then the defense counsel must be one, too. In both the general and special court-martial, however, the person on trial has the right to be represented by a qualified lawyer at government expense.

For a minor offense, such as a short absence without leave, there is the summary court-martial. This court has only one member, an officer, and it tries enlisted men and women. The summary court-martial does not require a counsel for either the prosecution or the defense.

Nonjudicial punishment, usually referred to as an Article 15, is handed out by the commanding officer. It could be for an offense such as not getting a haircut after repeated warnings.

## The "G.I. Supreme Court"

The final judge of law in the armed forces is usually the U.S. Court of Military Appeals. This "G.I. Supreme Court" has three civilian judges. (G.I., an abbreviation for "government issue," is sometimes used to refer to people in the armed forces.)

A court-martial is a military court called together under the authority of the government and the Uniform Code of Military Justice. The court-martial is used for trying and punishing offenses committed by members of the armed forces in violation of the Uniform Code of Military Justice.

From time to time, however, the U.S. Supreme Court does review military cases. In recent years, the Court has even issued several major decisions in military law.

## The Militia

For people in the militia, things are different. But what is the militia? This is the group of civilians at the state and local level who train regularly. In one sense, it is those persons in the reserves and National Guard who may be called up in case of an emergency. An example of such an emergency is the 1990 invasion of Kuwait by Iraqi forces. In a broader sense, though, the militia is all citizens who are fit to be called to military duty.

The militia falls under the military court system only "when in actual service in time of War or public danger." (Those who are on active duty in the armed forces are always under the military court system.) At other times, the militia falls under the civil court system.

Another question may occur when reading this section of the Fifth Amendment ("except in cases arising in the land or naval forces"). What is the exception?

The exception occurs when a person is on active duty. Then he or she is no longer a civilian and can therefore be tried in military courts. During wartime, there is another exception. Then, both private citizens and enemy soldiers who have violated the laws of war can be tried by a military commission.

## "The Case of the Saboteurs"

"The Case of the Saboteurs" started to unfold in June 1942. At that time, eight youths trained in sabotage and working for Nazi Germany were dropped off by German submarines along the coasts of Florida and Long Island. Dressed as civilians, they were soon picked up by the FBI in New York City and in Chicago. They were tried by a military commission for not wearing uniforms to show their combat status. The military commission looked for a precedent to help them decide the case. A precedent is a previous decision of a court. A precedent is used as an example or powerful reason for a decision in a new case that is similar in facts or legal principles. To find precedent for this trial, the members of the commission went all the way back to the 1780 trial of Major John André. André was a British officer who had been captured and hanged for spying during the Revolution.

"The Case of the Saboteurs" helped set up law for the gray area between civilian and military courts. It stated the right "to authorize the trial by court-martial of the members of the armed forces for all that class of crimes which under the Fifth and Sixth Amendments might otherwise have been deemed [believed] triable in the civil courts."

## The Case of General Tomoyuki Yamashita

At the end of World War II, another U.S. military commission tried a general of the Japanese armed forces. General Tomoyuki Yamashita was sentenced to death in 1946 for not preventing his troops from committing war crimes at Luzon in the Philippines. (Japan had overrun the Philippines in 1942.) However, it was not only unusual to try a soldier of the enemy. It was also unusual to try an enemy officer for what he did *not* do.

General Yamashita was even denied the due process of a fair trial. Not enough time was allowed for the preparation of the defense. Hearsay evidence was permitted as fact. Hearsay includes certain statements made outside the legal proceedings. A witness gives hearsay evidence when he or she tells not what he or she knows personally but what others have told him or her, or when the witness tells what he or she has heard said by others. There was no cross-examination of witnesses. It was never established that Yamashita knew of the war crimes. The lawyers appointed to defend Yamashita were not even allowed to raise constitutional questions. All this was at a trial that can be clearly viewed in light of the Fifth Amendment.

Justice Frank Murphy, one of the two Supreme Court justices who dissented from, or disagreed with, the majority finding of the commission trying General Yamashita, wrote:

> The Fifth Amendment guarantee of due process of law applies to "any person" who is accused of a crime by the Federal Government or any of its agencies. No exception is made as to those who are

General Tomoyuki Yamashita had commanded the Japanese campaign in the Philippines during World War II. He was tried by a U.S. military commission and was executed for atrocities.

accused of war crimes or as to those who possess the status of an enemy belligerent [fighter]. Indeed, such an exception would be contrary to the whole philosophy of human rights which makes the Constitution the great living document that it is.

But it was right after the war, and many people called out for the punishment of Japan and its leaders. Yamashita was condemned to death and hanged as a war criminal.

## The Armed Forces as an Exception

For most of its history, the U.S. Supreme Court has had a hands-off attitude toward the armed forces. Eighty years before the case of General Yamashita, Chief Justice Salmon P. Chase had written an opinion supporting the hands-off approach. In the *Milligan* case of 1866, Chase stated that "the power of Congress, in the government of the land and naval forces, is not affected by the Fifth or any other amendment."

Justice Robert H. Jackson, on the Court from 1941 to 1954, also understood the separateness of military life. "The military constitutes a specialized community governed by a separate discipline from that of the civilian," Jackson once wrote. "Orderly government requires that the judiciary be as scrupulous [careful] not to interfere with legitimate Army matters as the Army must be scrupulous not to intervene in judicial matters."

By the 1960s, the Supreme Court had limited the power of the UCMJ. Some of these restrictions were summarized in the decision in *O'Callahan* v. *Parker* (1969). "Discharged soldiers cannot be court-martialed for offenses committed while in service. . . . Neither civilian employees of the Armed Forces overseas . . . nor civilian dependants of military personnel accompanying them overseas . . . may be tried by court-martial." And finally, the decision stated something that might affect many soldiers on foreign land thousands of miles from home. A "crime to be under military jurisdiction must be service connected."

More than one hundred years after Chief Justice Chase's 1866 opinion in the *Milligan* case, the Court made a complete turn-around. The about-face came in 1967 in *United States* v. *Tempia*. The Military Court of Appeals ruled that the *Miranda* warnings, prohibiting forced confessions, also applied to military persons. Military justice was staying in step with the Fifth Amendment.

# CHAPTER 4

# Double Jeopardy

" . . . nor shall any person be subject for the same offence to be twice put in jeopardy of life or limb . . . "

THE FIFTH AMENDMENT

"**F**ear . . . of governmental power to try people twice for the same conduct is one of the oldest ideas found in western civilization," observed Justice Hugo L. Black. "Its roots run deep into Greek and Roman times. Even in the Dark Ages [from about A.D. 476 to 1350], when so many other principles of justice were lost, the idea that one trial and one punishment were enough remained alive through the canon [church] law and the teachings of the early Christian writers.

"By the thirteenth century it seems to have been firmly established in England, where it came to be considered as a 'universal maxim of the common law.' It is not surprising, therefore," wrote Justice Black in his dissenting opinion in *Bartkus* v. *Illinois* (1959),

> that the principle [of one trial and one punishment] was brought to this country by the earliest settlers as part of their heritage of freedom, and that it has been recognized here as fundamental again

---

Justice Benjamin N. Cardozo served on the Supreme Court from 1932 to 1938. In *Palko* v. *Connecticut* (1937), he wrote the majority opinion, which ruled against Palko's appeal to be protected against double jeopardy in a state trial. Yet Cardozo did recognize that some of the rights in the Bill of Rights should be protected against state actions.

and again. Today it is found, in varying forms, not only in the Federal Constitution, but in the jurisprudence [court decisions] or constitutions of every State, as well as most foreign nations. Few principles have been more deeply "rooted in the traditions and conscience of our people."

*Jeopardy* comes from the Old French words *jeu parti*, meaning "divided game." Jeopardy was a term used in games, particularly chess, when both sides had an equal chance of success or failure. The word thus became associated with a state of uncertainty. Later, the meaning expanded to include risk, danger, death, and injury.

Even older than the grand jury system is the concept of a person being "twice put in jeopardy." This means that a person is tried twice for the same offense, now commonly referred to as *double jeopardy*. A prohibition anchored in Roman law, it was even mentioned in ancient Greek writings. Before looking at the history of this concept, however, first examine the clause referring to double jeopardy as it appears in the Fifth Amendment.

The clause in the Fifth Amendment reads: "nor shall any person be subject for the same offence to be twice put in jeopardy of life or limb." This refers to serious crimes as well as serious punishments. "Put in jeopardy of life" could mean hanging or drowning or beheading, once common punishments for serious crimes.

The phrase "Put in jeopardy of . . . limb" might remind some readers of the awful medieval practice of "drawing and quartering" criminals for the crime of treason. (The criminal was hanged until he or she was almost dead, then drawn, or disemboweled, and the entrails thrown on a fire. Finally, the head was cut off, and the body was quartered, or divided into four parts. This brutal form of execution was finally outlawed in England in 1870.) However, the phrase more likely referred to the prohibition of other cruel punishments that had been used earlier in England. For instance, as punishment, people sometimes had their ears cut off and their tongues cut out for defying the Crown over their religious beliefs. Yet, as brutal punishments became rare, it was not long before

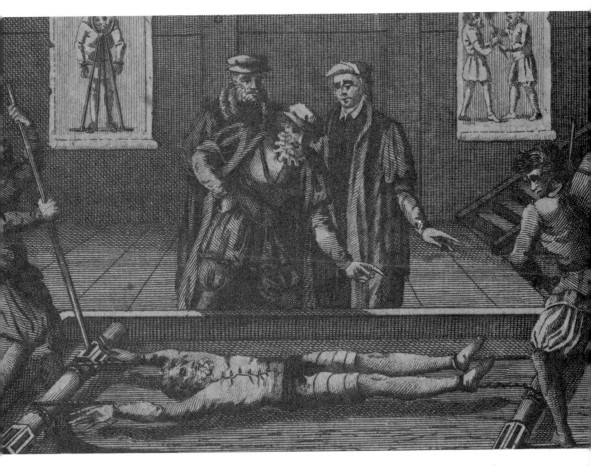

The rack was one form of medieval torture. The victim's body was stretched by ropes attached to the limbs.

"limb" developed a more symbolic meaning. It came to mean a prohibition of any punishment, less than life-ending, that came as a result of double jeopardy.

In the 1700s, the legal scholar Sir William Blackstone wrote *Commentaries on the Laws of England*. In it, he stated what he called "the universal maxim . . . that no man is to be brought into jeopardy of his life, more than once, for the same offence." Today, in English law, a person cannot be tried twice for the same offense. This is true whether the judgment is guilty or innocent.

In U.S. law, the prohibition against double jeopardy is more far-reaching and at the same time less precise than that in English law.

It includes the English idea of a person not being tried for the same offense again after an acquittal (being found not guilty) or a conviction. But the prohibition of double jeopardy does not apply if there has been no verdict in a case, as in a hung jury. A hung jury is a jury unable to reach a verdict. The person can be retried.

## Applying the Protection Against Double Jeopardy to the States

Up until the mid-1920s, justices on the Supreme Court had interpreted the Bill of Rights as protection against actions by the federal government. The Bill of Rights did not protect citizens from most actions taken against them by their state or local governments. States had their own bills of rights. Such a state bill of rights was supposed to protect its citizens if, for example, the state government tried to limit their right to free speech.

In 1925, the Supreme Court decided to use part of the Fourteenth Amendment (ratified in 1868) to change this way of understanding the Bill of Rights. The Supreme Court used the due process clause of the Fourteenth Amendment to make the First Amendment right of freedom of speech apply to the states. Over the next several decades, interpretations of the Fourteenth Amendment by some of the justices changed. They believed that those people who had ratified the Fourteenth Amendment had wanted all—or at least some—of the rights listed in the Bill of Rights to apply to the states. From the 1920s onward, more and more of the rights in the Bill of Rights have been incorporated, or made to apply to the states. Incorporation is the process of making the rights in the Bill of Rights apply to the states so that people are guaranteed to be safeguarded against state actions that might violate their rights.

The following question soon arose: Did the Fifth Amendment right to protection against double jeopardy apply to state trials as it already did to federal trials? The due process clause of the Fourteenth Amendment stated: "nor shall any State deprive any person of life, liberty, or property, without due process of law." Would the protection against double jeopardy be considered part of "due process of law" at the state level? If so, the states could not legally try a person twice for the same crime.

The matter came up in the important 1937 case of *Palko* v. *Connecticut*. The details of the case are as follows: Frank Palko had been indicted on a charge of first-degree murder of two police officers. If found guilty of first-degree murder, Palko could be sentenced to death. But the jury found him guilty of second-degree murder. He was sentenced to life imprisonment. The state of Connecticut appealed the conviction to a higher court. The state said that the indictment had charged Palko with first-degree murder. The state claimed there had been an error of law. The higher state court reversed the lower court's judgment and ordered a new trial. The jury at the new trial found Palko guilty of first-degree murder. The judge then sentenced him to death. Palko appealed the case to the Supreme Court. He claimed that double jeopardy—an action forbidden by the Fifth Amendment at the federal level—also is forbidden to the states by the Fourteenth Amendment.

Would the Supreme Court incorporate the Fifth Amendment's right to protection against double jeopardy? Would citizens be protected against being tried twice in state courts for the same crime? In *Palko* v. *Connecticut* (1937), the Supreme Court decided against Palko.

Justice Benjamin N. Cardozo wrote the Supreme Court's majority opinion. He stated that among the rights listed in the Bill of Rights some were so basic that they were "of the very essence of the scheme of ordered liberty." Such was freedom of speech. Others were not as basic. Among these not-so-basic rights was the protection against double jeopardy. "The state is not attempting to wear the accused out by a multitude of cases with accumulated [many] trials. It asks no more than this, that the case against him [Palko] shall go on until there shall be a trial free from the corrosion of substantial legal error."

The state carried out its execution of Palko. He was executed by electrocution.

## Double Jeopardy in Modern Times

An intriguing aspect of the prohibition against double jeopardy is how its basic ideas still seem to be open to different views. In 1969, the Supreme Court ruled that a state could *not* retry a criminal case that had already been tried in the federal courts. In the case of *Benton* v. *Maryland* (1969), the justices on the U.S. Supreme Court stated that "the double jeopardy prohibition of the Fifth Amendment represents a fundamental ideal in our constitutional heritage." The justices for the majority went on to state that "the same constitutional standards apply against both the State and Federal Governments." Thus, the case of *Benton* v. *Maryland* overturned the views expressed in the 1937 case of *Palko* v. *Connecticut*. The right to protection against double jeopardy was incorporated.

## The Supreme Court Today

The U.S. Supreme Court continues to look closely at different parts of the prohibition against double jeopardy. The process is called judicial review and is mainly focused on four elements: (1) When does double jeopardy begin in a case? (2) Can the accused be tried for the same crime by federal, state, and local governments? (3) How is double jeopardy affected by a breakdown of the charge into its different parts? (4) What is the effect of an appeal?

## When Double Jeopardy Begins

The basic question is, When does double jeopardy begin in a case? This is not a consideration during a grand jury or preliminary hearing. Only after an actual trial begins does double jeopardy start, or "attach" itself. But when does that moment occur?

What is now called "the lynchpin for all double jeopardy jurisprudence" is the decision in the case of *Crist* v. *Bretz* (1978). In both state and federal trials, this decision established double jeopardy as attaching itself right *after* the jury has been sworn in. If a trial is being held with only a judge and not a jury, double jeopardy "attaches" itself when the first witness is sworn in.

An interesting forerunner of this case took place in 1975 in *Breed et al* v. *Jones*. The trial of the defendant (Breed, a juvenile offender) had begun in juvenile court and was later transferred to adult court. The defendant successfully claimed that the transfer from one court to another was double jeopardy. The moment the juvenile court began to hear the facts in the case was the moment the trial began. It was not a situation of a continuation of the original case, as the prosecution claimed. Rather, it was a second trial for the same offense.

An exception to the prohibition against double jeopardy occurs in a trial that does not reach an outcome because the prosecution or the judge has made a mistake or has willingly done something wrong. In either instance, the trial ends in a mistrial because of "manifest necessity." It may then be possible to have a new trial. Another example of "manifest necessity" would be a problem caused by the state or federal government that helps the prosecution's case. If this happens, the defendant can refuse to undergo a new trial.

## Retrials by Federal, State, or Local Courts

In the case of *Bartkus* v. *Illinois* (1959), the question about double jeopardy came up in the following way. Bartkus, the defendant, had been tried in a federal court for robbing a federally insured savings and loan association. Bartkus was found innocent. He was then tried in a state court for the same crime and found guilty. Had his retrial for the same crime violated his right to protection against double jeopardy? The U.S. Supreme Court's 5-to-4 decision in the *Bartkus* case stated that the prohibition against double jeopardy did not apply if someone found not guilty at the federal level is then tried at the state level for the same crime under state law. (In another case in 1959, the Supreme Court also said that a federal trial could follow a state trial for the same offense.)

As might be expected, the Supreme Court's *Bartkus* v. *Illinois* decision met with an outcry of protest. For isn't this an example of "the state with all its resources and power" making "repeated attempts to convict an individual for an alleged offense" if a defendant is tried again and again? Isn't this "enhancing the possibility . . . [that the defendant] may be found guilty"? Or, as dissenting Justice William J. Brennan, Jr., once stated: "What happened here was simply that the federal effort which failed in the federal courthouse was renewed a second time in the state courthouse across the street."

Another dissenting justice, Hugo L. Black, addressed the problem when he observed: "The Court . . . takes the position that a second trial for the same act is somehow less offensive if one of the trials is conducted by the Federal Government and the other by a State. Looked at from the standpoint of the individual who is being prosecuted, this notion is too subtle for me to grasp."

Another question arose when a person was tried at both the state level and the local level. Can a person be tried for the same crime by both a local court—for example, a city or county court—and by a state court? In the case of *Waller* v. *Florida* (1970), the Court ruled that local units of government receive their power from the state to make local rules and laws. Therefore, people cannot undergo separate trials for the same crime by the state and by a local government of the same state. But a 1985 decision allowed one state to retry a person for the same crime he was tried for in a state court of a different state.

## The Breakdown of Charges into Different Parts

Many crimes today are very complex. They may best be dealt with when broken down into smaller parts. Each part of a criminal action might violate a different law. This is often true for crimes involving illegal drugs. Then separate trials with separate punishments can be held for each one.

As Robert E. Knowlton has observed:

A prosecutor, by carving up what is essentially one criminal transaction into a great number of offenses, may prosecute a person until the statute of limitations [time limit for enforcing a law] has run its course. This is true even though each trial may result in an acquittal and the only reason for the cumulative [additional] prosecutions is the prosecutor's subjective evaluation of the guilt of the individual.

There are limitations, however, in the dividing up of a criminal activity into many crimes to be tried separately. In a 1932 ruling, the Court said that "to determine whether there are two offenses or only one" it is necessary that each so-called crime "requires proof of an additional fact which the other does not."

## The Effect of an Appeal

The government does not usually appeal a sentence if there has been a fair trial. In the words of Justice Felix Frankfurter, the government does not retry cases "in order to allow a prosecutor who has been incompetent or casual or ineffective to see if he cannot do better a second time."

However, the Organized Crime Control Act of 1970 states that the federal government may appeal the sentences of "dangerous special offenders." Also, as in the decision in the case of *United States* v. *DiFrancesco* (1980), the U.S. Supreme Court stated that increasing sentences after judicial review is not in violation of the Fifth Amendment protection against double jeopardy.

Perhaps it goes without saying, though, that if a defendant does appeal, then a second trial does not violate the rights of the defendant against double jeopardy.

# The People's Right Against Self-Incrimination

"No person . . . shall be compelled in any criminal case to be a witness against himself. . . ."

THE FIFTH AMENDMENT

After the First Amendment (which guarantees freedom of religion, speech, and the press and the rights of assembly and petition), the Fifth Amendment may be the best-known amendment in the entire Bill of Rights.

The major reason why people are so familiar with the Fifth Amendment is based on fourteen words: " . . . nor shall be compelled in any criminal case to be a witness against himself." Forced self-incrimination is not allowed. This means that people have the right to remain silent. They cannot be forced to testify against themselves. Nor can Americans be forced to provide evidence against themselves. It is up to the government to accuse and then to prove guilt. The defendant cannot be forced to help the government in this task.

People are sometimes angered when they read or hear about a witness who "pleads the Fifth," that is, refuses to answer questions because the answers may lead to self-incrimination. They are viewing silence as a sign of guilt. They are making the assumption that if a witness will not talk freely he or she has something to hide.

---

King John of England signs Magna Carta at Runnymede in 1215. Early versions of several Fifth Amendment rights can be found in Magna Carta.

Of course there *are* present-day criminals who hide behind the Fifth Amendment. But as you will find out in this chapter, the growth of the right not to testify against oneself was a long battle.

## A Look Back

The Fifth Amendment reaches far back into history. Its origins can be traced to Magna Carta in 1215, as well as to Anglo-Saxon law before the Norman Conquest of Britain in 1066. (Justice Oliver Wendell Holmes once noted that "the rational study of law is . . . to a large extent the study of history.") Magna Carta is a document limiting the powers of the king. It grew out of the struggles of the English nobles against King John. Magna Carta serves as the symbolic cornerstone of English law, as well as a starting point for the American legal system.

## The Effects of the Inquisition

One of the worst examples of what can happen without a safeguard against self-incrimination took place during the Inquisition (a former Roman Catholic court). During the thirteenth century, Pope Innocent III revived this system of questioning heretics (people who differed from church doctrine). In addition to physical torture, the chief instrument for obtaining information was the *ex officio* oath. (*Ex officio* means "by virtue of an office." Because of his office, the questioner has the authority to demand answers. The oath that was taken by the person to be questioned was as follows: "You shall swear to answer all such interrogatories [questions] as shall be offered unto you and declare your whole knowledge therein, so God help you.") Sworn to tell the truth, people were then asked questions. The person under questioning often did not know what, if anything, he or she might be charged with.

The purpose of the methods used during the Inquisition was for the person to incriminate himself or herself. As a matter of fact, the person's testimony was often the sole basis of the charges. As a result, if the questioner was clever, the answers obtained would be more useful. Why? Because the answers would present a wider range of possibilities of proving wrongdoing later. But what if the person refused to answer any questions? Then it would be assumed that he or she was guilty. It was no wonder that above the doorway to the Roman court was the warning: "Abandon all hope, ye who enter here."

This was the infamous background of the *ex officio* oath that Pope Gregory IX introduced to England in 1236. For the next few hundred years, the oath and the methods of the Inquisition were often used by both the church and the government.

The Spanish Inquisition, Madrid. This is a scene of the pronouncement of judgment of the Inquisition. It was followed by the execution of sentence—the burning of heretics—by the government. One Inquisition method of questioning the accused was the use of the *ex officio* oath. The person's own testimony was often used as the evidence of his or her guilt.

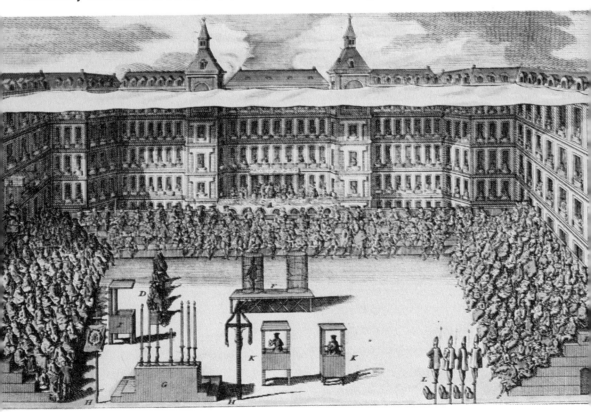

## The Accusatory System

Another legal tradition that existed in England had first grown in prominence during the reign of Henry II in the twelfth century. This was the accusatory system. One of the basic ideas of the system is found in these Latin words: *Nemo tenetur prodere seipsum.* This means that "no man is bound to accuse himself."

Although this system means that a person does not have to testify against himself or herself, it holds an even broader meaning. The burden of proof is *not* on the individual. It is not up to the individual to prove that he or she is innocent. Rather, it is up to the government to prove that the individual is guilty. The distance between these two positions is vast.

## The Legacies of Two Great Lawyers

One person who played a major role in the development of the law was Sir Edward Coke. Coke (pronounced COOK) had been the attorney general for England's Queen Elizabeth I and later King James I. After a career of working for the Crown and prosecuting its enemies, Coke in 1606 was named chief justice of the Court of Common Pleas. Once a judge, though, Coke acted differently. He started to speak out in favor of the rights of the individual.

But even with pressure from James I and an appointment as chief justice of the Court of King's Bench (an attempt to lessen his influence), Coke did not change his course. One of his main causes was to champion the role of Magna Carta as the basis for the law of the land. "Magna Carta is such a fellow," Coke said, "that he will have no sovereign." By the time Coke had finally been relieved of his duties in 1616, the right against self-incrimination was beginning to be recognized.

Another seventeenth-century English lawyer and scholar, John Selden, also advanced the cause against self-incrimination. "A man may plead not guilty, and yet tell no lie," observed Selden, "for by the law no man is bound to accuse himself."

Sir Edward Coke (1552–1634) became chief justice of important English courts and opposed King James I on a number of occasions. Coke fought to maintain basic English rights, including the right against self-incrimination.

John Selden was also important in advancing the accusatory system of justice over that of the Inquisition. "So when I say, Not guilty, the meaning is as if I should say by way of paraphrase, I am not so guilty as to tell you," wrote Selden. "If you will bring me to trial and have me punished for this you lay to my charge; prove it against me."

## The Champion of Liberty

But the person usually credited with doing the most to end the requirement of testifying against oneself is John Lilburne. In 1637, Lilburne was arrested for bringing Puritan pamphlets into England. He was ordered to appear before the Privy Council in the Star Chamber.

The Star Chamber, a courtroom named for the stars painted on the ceiling, was the meeting place for the king's councillors, or advisers. It was a faster and less rigid court than other courts because it did not operate according to common law. Other characteristics of the Star Chamber were that it did not use the jury system. It accepted rumor as truth. It could apply torture to obtain answers. And it could inflict any punishment short of death. The Star Chamber became the object of opposition from the lawyers in Parliament.

"I am not willing to answer you to any more of these questions," said Lilburne, "because I see you go about this Examination to ensnare [trap] me: for seeing the things for which I am imprisoned cannot be proved against me, you will get other matter out of my examination."

For not taking the *ex officio* oath, the twenty-three-year-old Lilburne was whipped. Even with his back bleeding, he continued to speak out against the injustice of this requirement. "It is an oath against the law of the land . . . the law of God; for that law requires no man to accuse himself; but if anything be laid to this charge, there must come two or three witnesses at least to prove it."

"[T]his Oath is against the very law of nature," Lilburne told those around him, "for nature is always a preserver of itself, and not a destroyer: But if a man takes this wicked oath, he undoes and destroys himself."

Again and again over the next three years, Lilburne was jailed, fined, and tortured. In his own words, he was "an honest true-bred, freeborn Englishman that never in his life loved a tyrant nor feared

Coll. IOHN LILBORNE.

John Lilburne (about 1614–1657) was repeatedly imprisoned in England. He fought against the *ex officio* oath and forced self-incrimination.

an oppressor." As the opponents of Charles I came to the aid of this champion of freedom whom they called "Freeborn John," the government became more and more isolated.

With Coke's law books at his side, John Lilburne acted as his own defense attorney. Lilburne was known for being able to outtalk anyone in the courtroom. In fact, it was once said that even if John Lilburne were the only person left in the world, there would not be silence. John would be heard arguing with Lilburne, and Lilburne would be heard arguing with John.

Not only was he a master talker, he also produced many pamphlets. Once one of his trials was recessed. Before it could be started again, copies of *The Exceptions of John Lilburne to a Bill of Indictment*, his latest pamphlet, were being handed out in the streets.

Finally in 1641 the House of Commons, the lower house of Parliament, issued a proclamation "That the Sentence of the Star-Chamber given against John Lilburn[e] is illegal, and against the Liberty of the subject; and also bloody, cruel, wicked, barbarous, and tyrannical."

It was not long afterward that the House of Lords, the upper house of Parliament, followed. The official announcement stated that his sentence was "illegal, and most unjust, against the liberty of the subject and law of the land, and Magna Charta." The Star Chamber was done away with by Parliament that same year.

These rulings may not have healed the scars across Lilburne's back. Nor did they lessen the hardship of his struggle against the government over the next twenty years. However, thousands of people—from the seventeenth century to the present day—can be grateful to John Lilburne. For this brave man, who died in prison, helped to establish the right to remain silent.

## The Trial of Anne Hutchinson

One person who did not benefit from the work of John Lilburne was on the other side of the Atlantic Ocean in the Massachusetts

Bay Colony. In 1637, at about the same time that Lilburne was beginning his trials, Anne Hutchinson was being tried in America. Hutchinson had held popular religious meetings in her home and had opposed the authority of the church and its ministers. Without counsel and under the guidance of Governor John Winthrop,

The trial of Anne Hutchinson in Boston, 1637. She preached the importance of the individual's sensing God's grace and love without regard for obedience to specific laws of the church and colony. She was tried and convicted for "traducing [injuring the reputation of] the ministers and ministry." Hutchinson was forced to leave the Massachusetts Bay Colony.

Hutchinson was led to incriminate herself as forty church leaders listened in judgment.

"Now if you condemn me for speaking what in my conscience I know to be truth," said Hutchinson, "I must commit myself unto the Lord."

The verdict of the church leaders was stern: "You are banished from out of our jurisdiction as being a woman not fit for our society, and are to be imprisoned until the court shall send you away."

As William H. Moody, a justice of the U.S. Supreme Court, would later observe about Governor Winthrop, "an examination of the report of this trial will show that he was not aware of any privilege against self-incrimination or conscious of any duty to respect it."

## Other Self-Incrimination Cases in Colonial America

Two other important cases of self-incrimination in colonial America took place in Pennsylvania and Massachusetts. In 1735, Benjamin Franklin heard that a minister in Philadelphia had been ordered to submit his sermons for church review. "It was contrary to the common Rights of Mankind," argued Franklin, "no Man being obliged to furnish Matter of Accusation against himself."

Another minister who was ordered to deliver a copy of a sermon was none other than the brother-in-law of Anne Hutchinson. His name was John Wheelwright. At a hearing before the General Court in 1637, Wheelwright was told he would be asked about his sermon. Wheelwright wanted to know if he was being questioned as an innocent person or as a guilty person. "Neither" was the reply. Then Wheelwright wanted to know who his accusers were. The court told him his sermon was. Then he was told that he was going to be questioned *ex officio*. At the very mention of that term, Wheelwright refused to answer any questions. Nevertheless, the court came to a decision. Like Anne Hutchinson, John Wheelwright was banished from Massachusetts.

## Changes During the Colonial Period

Not only could the rule of law be seen in the eighteenth century moving away from confession and self-incrimination. The rule of law could also be glimpsed heading toward the accusatory system of today. Also, the burden of proof was shifting away from the shoulders of the individual. Toward the close of the colonial period, the burden of proof was beginning to settle around the institution of government.

## A View from the Twentieth Century

Over three hundred years after Lilburne and Hutchinson, Justice Arthur J. Goldberg would write of the significance of the people's right against self-incrimination. His comments only add to the solid foundation that Coke, Selden, and Lilburne laid back in the 1600s.

The right to remain silent, noted Goldberg in 1964, "reflects many of our fundamental values and most noble aspirations: our unwillingness to subject those suspected of crime to the cruel trilemma [three difficult choices] of self-accusation, perjury or contempt."

# CHAPTER 6

# The People's Right Against Self-Incrimination to the Present Day

" . . . nor shall be compelled in any criminal case to be witness against himself . . ."

THE FIFTH AMENDMENT

As more and more English people left for the promise of better lives in America, they brought English common law with them. But there were instances in the colonies of abuses of the people's right of protection against forced self-incrimination. The most famous was the Salem witchcraft trials.

The witchcraft hysteria of 1692 was started by ten girls ranging in age from nine to seventeen. During the winter, these girls learned about "magic" from a West Indian woman, the slave of the village minister. They heard the local tale-telling about witches. Within four months, hundreds of people in Salem Village and elsewhere had been accused of witchcraft. Not only were witnesses not allowed to remain silent, they were also subject to psychological and physical punishment to obtain confessions. In all, nineteen people were hanged. One was even pressed to death when he refused to plead when accused. Not until leading citizens outside of Salem had been accused was the witch-hunt brought to a halt.

During the 1700s, few records of trial proceedings were kept. However, the people's right of protection against forced self-

---

The Salem witchcraft trials, 1692, are a colonial example of forced self-incrimination. Witchcraft trials were common in Europe.

incrimination received prominent mention in law books. The most widely used book for justices of the peace was *Conductor Generalis*. It stated "a general rule, that a witness shall not be asked any question, the answering of which might oblige him to accuse himself of a crime."

Near the close of the Constitutional Convention, on September 12, 1787, George Mason, a delegate from Virginia, said that he "wished the plan had been prefaced by a Bill of Rights." He knew that a bill of rights "would give great quiet to the people." However, most of the delegates did not feel there was a need for one. Besides, after a long summer of hard work, they were eager to leave Philadelphia for their homes.

George Mason had helped write the Virginia Declaration of Rights in 1776. This document granted protection against self-incrimination ("nor can he be compelled to give evidence against himself") for the accused person in Virginia. Other states had soon followed. They drew up their own constitutions guaranteeing rights against self-incrimination to their citizens. But people from the different states became anxious about the lack of a bill of rights in the Constitution of the United States. As George Mason said, "The laws of the United States are to be paramount to state bills of rights."

In 1789, James Madison wrote and fought for a bill of rights. That is why Madison is known today as "the father of the Bill of Rights."

Madison patterned the Fifth Amendment after the Virginia Declaration of Rights. His first version of the self-incrimination clause read: "nor shall be compelled to be a witness against himself." However, the U.S. House of Representatives added the words "in any criminal case."

Because of this addition, it was first believed that the right of a person to remain silent existed only in criminal cases. But the right applies to civil cases as well. Civil cases concern all those cases involving noncriminal actions, such as legal disputes about property and private rights and lawsuits dealing with personal injury. In

George Mason of Virginia is noted for his part in writing the Virginia Declaration of Rights of 1776. James Madison used parts of this document when writing the amendments that became known as the Bill of Rights.

fact, it now includes almost every situation that a person might be in. As Justice Lewis F. Powell stated in 1971: "It [a person's right to remain silent] can be asserted in any proceeding civil or criminal, administrative or judicial, investigative or adjudicatory; and it protects any disclosures [statements] that the witness reasonably believes could be used in a criminal prosecution or could lead to other evidence that might be so used."

One case that attempted to standardize an aspect of trials involving the people's right against self-incrimination was *Brown*

v. *Walker* (1896). The decision in this case stated that if a defendant took the stand to speak on his or her own behalf, then the right to remain silent was no longer an option. The defendant was open to a cross-examination by the prosecutor.

However, the practice of letting the states have the final word in trials that involved self-incrimination was firmly established in 1908 by the decision in *Twining* v. *New Jersey*. In this case the U.S. Supreme Court ruled that the Fifth Amendment did not keep a state from forcing a person to testify. In other words, the Fifth Amendment guarantee against forced self-incrimination did not protect citizens against state action.

It was not until 1964 that the hold of states' rights was loosened. In the decision in *Malloy* v. *Hogan*, the Supreme Court declared: "We hold that the Fourteenth Amendment guarantees the petitioner the protection of the Fifth Amendment's privilege against self-incrimination." The right to protection against forced self-incrimination was applied to the states. The right was incorporated.

## The Witch-Hunt of Joseph McCarthy

Over 250 years after the Salem witchcraft trials, another kind of witch-hunt took place. Joseph McCarthy, a senator from Wisconsin, charged that the U.S. government was being taken over by Communists. Between 1950 and 1954, McCarthy held hearing after hearing, and scores of witnesses were called to testify.

One of McCarthy's favorite techniques was to find out the type of question that would cause the witness to call upon the rights guaranteed by the Fifth Amendment. Then McCarthy would ask follow-up questions of a similar nature. Before long it would appear that the witness was trying to hide behind the Fifth Amendment. (Some of the witnesses refused to answer questions but also refused to call upon the rights guaranteed by the Fifth Amendment. They called upon the rights guaranteed by the First Amendment and were consequently jailed.) Although McCarthy seldom presented any valid evidence to back up his many charges, the hearings received full coverage in newspapers and on television.

In late 1953, McCarthy began looking for Communists in the army. The army filed countercharges, and a special U.S. Senate hearing was held to investigate this issue. The hearing was carried live on television. Millions of Americans watched as McCarthy made unsupported charges. After the lengthy hearing, the U.S. Senate publicly condemned McCarthy for his reckless conduct. By that time, though, the careers and good names of many people had been ruined. McCarthy's tactics and his way of seeing the devil of communism everywhere even gave rise to the term *McCarthyism.*

Senator Joseph R. McCarthy (right) with his assistant Roy Cohn. McCarthy accused many people of subversive activities and gained much popular support for the investigations his Senate subcommittee carried on in the early 1950s. Some of the witnesses he called refused to answer his questions, citing their Fifth Amendment right against self-incrimination.

## The *Escobedo* Case

In 1964, the U.S. Supreme Court found by a 5-to-4 vote that a confession by a person in custody was not admissible evidence. Why? Because the murder suspect had repeatedly tried to contact his lawyer and had been repeatedly denied the right. As a matter of fact, the lawyer was even present at the police station and was trying to gain permission to see his client. This case of *Escobedo* v. *Illinois* was a Sixth Amendment right-to-counsel case. But it also involved the person's right against self-incrimination. (The decision spoke of Escobedo's "absolute right to remain silent.") *Escobedo* v. *Illinois* was one of the landmark cases of the century.

## The Importance of the *Miranda* Case

In 1966, the U.S. Supreme Court expanded the people's right against self-incrimination in its decision in *Miranda* v. *Arizona*. Ernesto Arthur Miranda, a twenty-three-year-old man, was arrested as a suspect in the kidnapping and rape of a teenager. After two hours in an interrogation room (a room where police can question witnesses and suspects) of the Phoenix police station, Miranda confessed.

The Supreme Court, however, in a 5-to-4 decision, ruled that Miranda's confession could not be used as evidence. The Court found that anyone arrested on suspicion of a crime must be told by the arresting officer of his or her right to remain silent and given the opportunity to have a lawyer present during questioning.

Chief Justice Earl Warren delivered the opinion of the Court. The ruling in the *Miranda* case reads in part:

> Prior to any questioning, the person must be warned that he has a right to remain silent, that any statement he does make may be used as evidence against him, and that he has a right to the presence of an attorney, either retained or appointed. The defendant may waive effectuation [the putting into effect] of these rights, provided the

waiver is made voluntarily, knowingly and intelligently. If, however, he indicates in any manner and at any stage of the process that he wishes to consult with an attorney . . . [or] . . . that he does not wish to be interrogated, the police may not question him.

Miranda was retried and found guilty. He was paroled and was eventually killed in a knife fight. The suspect in his murder was read the *Miranda* rights.

Before the *Miranda* case, there had been previous court cases dealing with the questioning environment. Physical and psychological abuse had sometimes been used to gain confessions from suspects. Five days of nonstop questioning by teams of officers, lawyers, and legal experts would almost always result in the breakdown of a defendant.

In questioning suspects, even the smallest police station would use the "good cop–bad cop" method. One interviewer—the "good cop"—would be understanding. But the other interviewer—the "bad cop"—would be tough. The two would alternate in questioning the individual. Sometimes, the "good cop" might even suggest a confession because he was afraid of what the "bad cop" might do to the accused.

The decision in the *Miranda* case dealt with the issue of cutting off the defendant from the outside world and using nonstop questioning. "It is obvious that such an interrogation environment is created for no purpose other than to subjugate the individual [force the person to give in] to the will of the examiner," wrote Chief Justice Earl Warren for the majority.

This atmosphere carries its own badge of intimidation. To be sure, this is not physical intimidation, but it is equally destructive of human dignity. The current practice of incommunicado interrogation [being cut off from the outside during questioning] is at odds with one of our nation's most cherished principles—that the individual may not be compelled to incriminate himself.

Today, the setting of an interrogation room in a police station includes the *Miranda* warnings that must be read to the suspect. To help an arresting officer maintain a suspect's rights, checklists based on the U.S. Supreme Court's ruling in the *Miranda* case were drawn up by police departments. A sample of what a police officer might read aloud to a suspect appears here.

### Warnings to Be Given to Persons in Police Custody Before Beginning Interrogation

1. "You have the right to remain silent and not answer any questions."
2. "Anything you say may be used against you in a court of law."
3. "You have the right to speak to a lawyer first. You may have a lawyer present now and during any future questioning."
4. "If you cannot afford a lawyer, you will be provided with one at no expense to you."
5. "If you do not have a lawyer at this time, you have the right to remain silent until you have had a chance to talk to one."
6. "Now that I have advised you about your rights, are you willing to answer any questions without a lawyer present?"

In thinking about the *Escobedo* and *Miranda* cases, it might be helpful to recall the plea made by John Lilburne during one of his many trials—during his trial for treason in 1649. "And now, Sir," Lilburne said, "I again desire counsel to be assigned to me, to consult with in point of law, that so I may not destroy myself through my ignorance."

## Types of Immunity

There are other situations today, however, when a person *can* be required to testify. One is if it is shown that the witness cannot possibly be prosecuted. This is known as *transactional immunity*. Another is if the statute of limitations (time limit for enforcement of a particular law) has expired, or run out. The person may also have to testify if he or she has been pardoned, is protected by the prohibition against double jeopardy, or has been granted immunity.

This last type of immunity is known as *use immunity*. Begun by the U.S. Congress, this type of immunity protects the witness against prosecution for certain testimony given. However, the witness may still be prosecuted for other aspects of the larger issue or transaction that were not dealt with in the sworn testimony.

One tactic that some prosecutors had used with success was banned in 1965 by the U.S. Supreme Court's decision in *Griffin* v. *California*. This decision stated that prosecutors and judges could not comment on the fact that a defendant did not take the stand. This would amount to a "penalty [being] imposed by courts [on a defendant] for exercising a constitutional privilege." It would seem to go against the whole point of a person's right to remain silent.

Not speaking in one's behalf is not the same as admitting guilt. There are many reasons why someone would not want to take the stand. (One, of course, could be that the person is guilty.) Not the least of these reasons might be that the prosecution may not have done a good job in proving its case. In such a case, there would be little sense in harming the outcome of the trial by having the defendant open up to a clever cross-examination. It's a bit like a football game. If a team is barely ahead at the close of the game, it can be better for that team to hang onto the ball and let the seconds tick down. Allowing the other team to get the ball will present the opportunity for the opposition to come from behind and win the game.

## Two Recent Rulings

Two U.S. Supreme Court rulings in 1990 have also had direct effects on the Fifth Amendment. In one case, the Court ruled that a videotape of a driver arrested for drunk driving could be entered as evidence at the trial. This was true even though the *Miranda* warnings had not been given and the driver's slurred speech was heard on the tape. However, the incriminating evidence, "the physical inability to articulate [state] words in a clear manner," was physical evidence rather than "testimonial." (For years, the Supreme Court has drawn the distinction between physical and "testimonial" evidence when interpreting a person's right against self-incrimination under the Fifth Amendment.)

In the other case, an inmate had bragged to another prisoner about a murder he had committed. The other prisoner, however, turned out to be an undercover officer. The Supreme Court found it permissible to use the undercover officer's testimony at a later trial.

## The Trial of Sir Thomas More

A prisoner may not be the most sympathetic individual possible. However, this depends upon the identity of the prisoner. At the trial of Sir Thomas More in 1535, the jury was about to vote for acquittal (freeing from charge). Suddenly, the solicitor general (a law officer who helps the attorney general), Richard Rich, resigned from his office, so that he could tell of his confidential conversation with More in the Tower of London.

"There were things which no parliament could do," Richard Rich recalled he had said to More that day in the Tower. "[For example,] . . . no parliament could make a law that God should not be God."

"No more could the parliament," Sir Thomas More had replied, "make the king supreme head of the Church."

After hearing Rich's testimony, the jury returned a verdict of guilty. More was found guilty of perjury—lying while under oath—as well as of refusing to swear to the oath of the Act of Supremacy. (This was an act of 1534 proclaiming that the king of England was also the head of the Church of England.) Before the week was over, Sir Thomas More was dead, his severed head displayed on London Bridge for all to see.

Sir Thomas More (1478–1535) was an English statesman and author. He quarreled with Henry VIII. More was convicted of treason for refusing to agree to the Act of Supremacy, which made the king the leader of the Church of England. More was beheaded.

In considering the Fifth Amendment in light of the present day, it might be useful to recall something that Chief Justice Earl Warren once wrote.

The privilege against self-incrimination is a right that was hard-earned by our forefathers. The reasons for its inclusion [being included] in the Constitution—and the necessities for its preservation—are to be found in the lessons of history. . . . To apply the privilege narrowly or begrudgingly—to treat it as a historical relic, at most merely to be tolerated—is to ignore its development and purpose.

# CHAPTER 7

# The Importance of Due Process

"No person shall . . . be deprived of life, liberty, or property, without due process of law. . . ."

THE FIFTH AMENDMENT

**W**hat is meant by the due process clause of the Fifth Amendment? Generally speaking, the due process of law stands for "essential fairness."

## The People's Rights of Due Process

Think of the people's rights of due process of law in terms of a criminal trial. Why? Because a criminal trial most clearly shows the procedures guaranteeing the people's rights of due process in action.

In order for a defendant to receive the due process of a fair trial, certain safeguards listed in the Bill of Rights must be honored. These are the rights stated in the Fifth Amendment: the right to a grand jury hearing, the protection against double jeopardy, the protection against self-incrimination. But due process also includes the rights listed in three other amendments in the Bill of Rights.

---

Chief Justice John Marshall served on the Supreme Court from 1801 to 1835. He was one of the main founders of the American system of constitutional law. In his majority opinion in *Marbury* v. *Madison* (1803), he set forth the idea of judicial review.

One of these is the right against "unreasonable searches and seizures" assured by the Fourth Amendment. Another is the "right to a speedy and public trial by an impartial jury" held in the area where the alleged crime was committed, as guaranteed by the Sixth Amendment. Also listed in the Sixth Amendment are the following: the right to be told of the crime one is charged with, the right to cross-examine witnesses, the right to have favorable witnesses, and the right to have a lawyer. And finally, there are the rights promised in the Eighth Amendment. These are the rights against excessive bail and fines, and the protection against "cruel and unusual" punishment.

The end result of a trial is that the jury either finds a defendant innocent or guilty. (There could also be a mistrial, as for example, when a jury cannot decide.) To be guilty, a defendant must be proved guilty beyond a reasonable doubt. This does not mean guilt by association or conduct that seems suspicious. The people's right of due process of law requires that a jury find a defendant guilty beyond a reasonable doubt.

## How Due Process Came into Being

Basic to our Constitution and legal system is the idea of due process of law. It comes to us from Magna Carta. This was a document that English nobles drew up and King John signed on June 15, 1215, at Runnymede near London. Chapter 39 contained the following statement: "No free man shall be taken or imprisoned or disseized [have his possessions taken away] or exiled or in any way destroyed, nor will we go upon him nor send upon him, except by the lawful judgment of his peers [equals] or by the law of the land."

The concept of "the law of the land" as stated in Magna Carta removed for the first time the absolute power of the ruler. No one could be punished by the Crown unless he or she had broken a law. This was the first stop on a road that would lead to our present-day democracy.

In 1354 the term *due process of law* was first mentioned in English law. During the reign of Edward III, Parliament passed a law that referred to the all-important "law of the land" chapter of Magna Carta. This law stated: "No man of what state [rank] or condition he be, shall be put out of his lands or tenements nor taken, nor disinherited, nor put to death, without he be brought to answer by due process of law."

Two later champions of the importance of due process were John Lilburne and Edward Coke. From 1637 to 1657, John Lilburne was jailed over and over again. He suffered extreme hardship in his fight for the right against self-incrimination. "Though I be pulled apart by wild horses," Lilburne said, he would never testify under the *ex officio* oath. It is "both against the law of God and the law of the land." Lilburne never gave up his belief that this right is one of the principles of due process of law.

For Sir Edward Coke, the law of the land meant common law. Common law was based on the decisions of judges in specific cases. It was the law that was used throughout the realm. "Reason is the life of the law," declared Coke, "nay, the common law is nothing else but reason."

Later, in 1628, Coke equated *law of the land* with *due process of law* while discussing the importance of Magna Carta. Nevertheless, it would still be some time before the two terms would have a similar meaning.

The term *due process of law* was also set up in Darnel's case in 1627. For refusing to pay a war tax called for by Charles I, five men were sent to jail. John Selden defended them in court. He stated: "No freeman shall be imprisoned without due process of law." In this instance, Selden's meaning of *due process of law* was "the presentment and indictment of the grand jury." (See Chapter 2.)

The term *law of the land,* however, was used more often than *due process of law.* This was true both in England and later in colonial America. As a matter of fact, the term *due process of law* was seldom mentioned in America until its appearance in the Fifth Amendment. Why did it show up there? The major reason seems to be because James Madison preferred it.

## The States' Bills of Rights

Magna Carta influenced not only the Bill of Rights of the federal government, but also the bill of rights of every state. The bills of rights of the first eight states to join the Union use the term *law of the land*. However, the Bill of Rights of the United States and the bills of rights of more recent states use the term *due process of law*.

## The Importance of Judicial Review

In 1801, near the end of President John Adams's administration, the U.S. Congress passed laws setting up over fifty new federal judgeships. Adams spent his last night as president signing the commissions of his "midnight judges." A commission is a special government document giving a person the power to hold a government office. It was John Marshall's job as outgoing secretary of state to deliver the commissions. Unfortunately for the Federalists, John Marshall overlooked delivering some of them. When Thomas Jefferson became president, he ordered James Madison, the new secretary of state, not to deliver the commissions. The new president did not want all those new judges faithful to the Federalists. Marbury, one of the appointees who had not received his commission, took Madison to court. Marbury asked the Supreme Court to issue a special order forcing Madison to hand over the commission. According to the Judiciary Act of 1789, the Supreme Court had the power to issue such a special order.

In 1803, in the case of *Marbury* v. *Madison,* the U.S. Supreme Court overruled an act of Congress. The Court declared part of the Judiciary Act of 1789 unconstitutional. Congress had no right to pass a law allowing the Supreme Court to issue such a special order. John Marshall, now chief justice of the United States and soon to become one of the most famous judges in American history, wrote the majority opinion on this important occasion.

> It is . . . the province and duty of the judicial department, to say what the law is. . . . If two laws conflict with each other, the courts must decide on the operation of each. . . . If then, the courts are to regard the constitution, and the constitution is superior to any ordinary act of the legislature, the constitution, and not such ordinary act, must govern the case to which they both apply.

The case of *Marbury* v. *Madison* saw the beginning of one of the most important jobs of the Supreme Court: judicial review. The Court reviews the acts of other branches of the government—when they apply to cases being considered by the Court. The Court's role is to find out whether or not these acts are constitutional. The decision in the *Marbury* case was the first time that the Court had overruled Congress. It would not occur again for over fifty years.

## A Judicial Review of Due Process

The Supreme Court of the United States dealt with the idea of due process of law for the first time in 1856. The case was *Murray's Lessee* v. *Hoboken Land and Improvement Co.* This case dealt with the constitutionality of placing a levy (amount of money legally to be collected) on a company in debt to the U.S. government.

To find out if due process was being followed, the Supreme Court first looked at the U.S. Constitution. If the elements in the case did not violate any of the provisions of the Constitution, the Court would next look at "those settled usages and modes of proceedings existing in the common and statute law of England, before the emigration of our ancestors. . . ." This led to the discovery that the English Crown had often recovered debts in this fashion.

Would this mean that due process was bound by the historical procedures of England and America? No, "it by no means follows that nothing else can be due process of law" was the ruling in the 1884 case of *Hurtado* v. *California*. California was giving up its use of the grand jury even though it was still "the law of the land" in England. In keeping up an effective due process of law, the U.S. Supreme Court ruled that it must pay close attention not to "particular forms of procedures, but [to] the very substance of individual rights to life, liberty, and property." Otherwise, the effect of the Court on due process "would be to deny every quality of the law but its age, and to render [make] it incapable of progress or improvement."

## The Importance of the *Dred Scott* Case

The next time that the U.S. Supreme Court overruled the U.S. Congress was in the decision in *Dred Scott* v. *Sandford* in 1857. This case had been in the courts a long time. Known first as *Scott, a Man of Color* v. *Emerson,* it was a case to test the legality of slavery. The slave Scott had been brought by his owner to live for a while in the free state of Illinois and in Wisconsin Territory. According to the Missouri Compromise passed by Congress in 1820, that territory did not allow slavery. Dred Scott was then brought back to the slave state of Missouri. Scott sued to gain his freedom.

In brief, the *Dred Scott* case, as it is called, dealt with three issues: (1) Did Scott have the right to sue in federal court? (2) Could Congress forbid the spread of slavery to the new territories? (3) Was the Missouri Compromise of 1820 unconstitutional?

Chief Justice Roger B. Taney (pronounced TAW-nee) wrote a decision that stated African Americans were not citizens when the U.S. Constitution had been adopted. Thus, they could not sue in federal court.

Answering the second question, Taney wrote that "the act of Congress which prohibited a citizen from holding and owning

Dred Scott sued to obtain his freedom. The Supreme Court ruled against him in the famous case of *Dred Scott* v. *Sandford* (1857). Soon after that ruling, Scott was sold to a new owner who freed him.

property of this kind in the territory of the United States north of the line therein mentioned, is not warranted by the Constitution, and is therefore void.''

Finally, in answer to the third question, Taney stated that ''an act of Congress which deprives a citizen of the United States of his liberty or property, merely because he came himself or brought his

Chief Justice Roger B. Taney served on the Supreme Court from 1836 to 1864. His majority opinion in the *Dred Scott* case aroused anger as the controversy over slavery grew in the years before the Civil War.

property into a particular territory of the United States, and who had committed no offense against the laws, could hardly be dignified with the name of due process of law."

In other words, African Americans were not citizens, Congress did not have the power to forbid the extension of slavery into a territory, and the Missouri Compromise of 1820 was unconstitutional.

The ruling in the *Dred Scott* case helped push the country toward Civil War. Abraham Lincoln, a candidate opposed to the introduction of slavery into the territories, went on to become president in 1860. As Lincoln once said to a Southerner: "You think slavery is *right* and ought to be extended; while we think it *wrong* and ought to be restricted. That I suppose is the rub."

Briefly stated, the slavery issue and keeping the Union together were the problems. So, in anticipation of further restrictions, the Southern states seceded from the Union.

There was another important outcome of the decision in the *Dred Scott* case. Since that ruling, judicial review by the Supreme Court of the laws of Congress has become common. Justice Oliver Wendell Holmes once said this about the process of judicial review: "I do not think the United States would come to an end if we lost our power to declare an Act of Congress void. [However,] I do think the Union would be imperiled [put in danger] if we could not make that declaration as to the laws of the several States."

After the Civil War, the Southern states were returned to the Union, and slavery was abolished. To make sure the 3 million African Americans who were now free would be treated equally wherever they lived, three amendments were passed immediately after the Civil War. The second one of these, adopted in 1868, was the Fourteenth Amendment.

The purpose of the Fourteenth Amendment was to guarantee that people would be treated fairly by all the states. The Fourteenth Amendment even uses words about due process (*nor shall any State deprive any person of life, liberty, or property, without due process of law*) that are similar to those found in the Fifth Amendment. From this time on, the term *due process of law* began to be used regularly in the United States.

## After the Civil War

The Civil War divided the country into two warring sides: the Union and the Confederacy. It also served as another kind of dividing line. Before the war, due process of law was mainly procedural. That means it involved the procedures, methods, or rules about how public officials carry out the law. For example, a question of procedural due process might be one asking whether someone had been unfairly denied a lawyer during a trial. Another might be whether a search and seizure of someone's home and property had been unreasonable. In the decades after the Civil War, due process became more and more substantive. That means it involved the actual content or subject matter of the laws. For example, a question of substantive due process might be whether a law of Congress could set maximum hours that children could work. In both procedural and substantive due process cases, the courts would ask whether an action of a public official or a law, in procedure or content, was unconstitutional.

## Due Process over the Years

The legal principle of due process of law is contained in a body of law that protects both people and institutions. As Justice Felix Frankfurter once wrote: "Representing as it does a living principle, due process is not confined within a permanent catalogue of what may at a given time be deemed the limits or essentials of fundamental rights."

This is true no matter what kind of due process it is—procedural or substantive. (For a discussion of procedural due process of law, the fair administration of laws, see Chapters 8 and 9. For a treatment of substantive due process of law, ensuring that laws are reasonable, see Chapter 10.)

The legal principle of due process of law may have had only a modest beginning in 1215 when King John signed Magna Carta. But over the years, due process of law has grown into one of the most important concepts in the U.S. Constitution.

# CHAPTER 8

# Procedural Due Process of Civil Law

"Someone must have been telling lies about Joseph K., for without having done anything wrong he was arrested one fine morning. . . ."

The Trial by FRANZ KAFKA

The importance of charges being made clear is shown in the beginning of *The Trial* by Franz Kafka. Joseph K., the main character, has no idea of what the charges are against him.

" 'Proceedings have been instituted against you,' " he is told, " 'and you will be informed of everything in due course.' "

The sleepless nightmare that Joseph K. finds himself in only worsens as time passes in this major twentieth-century work of fiction.

## Some Characteristics of Procedural Due Process of Civil Law

One of the important ways we have to prevent the nightmare of a Joseph K. situation is procedural due process of civil law. As Justice Felix Frankfurter noted, "The history of liberty is largely the observance of procedural safeguards." Here are some of these important safeguards:

---

A witness being questioned on the witness stand. The Fifth Amendment provides for due process of law. Included in the due process concept are the established rules for fair trials.

1. Charges must be made clear.

    It is necessary to tell people of the charges against them. Otherwise, people can be thrown into a situation similar to the one that Joseph K. found himself in.

2. Adequate notice needs to be given for a hearing.

    Closely associated with the necessity of telling people of the charges against them is the need for adequate notice. There should be no element of surprise in a hearing. All parties (people involved in the dispute) should have plenty of time so that they can be fully prepared.

3. A chance to present one's own case and refute (to prove wrong) an opponent's version must be given.

    Depending on the complexity and importance of the situation, there may be a chance to bring in evidence and witnesses. There may also be a right to cross-examine witnesses and a right to have a lawyer present.

4. A fair hearing before an impartial person must be given.

    This sense of fairness prevents charges being brought by the same person who will later judge the case. For to face someone who is a combination of accuser, judge, and jury plunges the defendant into a nightmarish situation.

## The Due Process Clauses

Now is the time to examine in detail the due process clauses of the Fifth and Fourteenth Amendments.

> . . . nor be deprived of life, liberty, or property, without due process of law . . .
>
> THE FIFTH AMENDMENT

> . . . nor shall any State deprive any person of life, liberty, or property, without due process of law . . .
>
> THE FOURTEENTH AMENDMENT

Both amendments forbid the depriving of "life, liberty, or property, without due process of law." The Fifth applies due process to the federal government. The Fourteenth Amendment applies due process to the states.

## Life, Liberty, or Property

The depriving of life concerns the *procedural due process of criminal law.* One cannot be legally subjected to harsh penalties unless the due process of law is followed as stated in the Fourth, Fifth, Sixth, and Eighth Amendments. This is particularly true when it comes to the most extreme penalty of all, capital punishment—the death penalty. Executions take place only after other approaches to possible exceptions have been closed.

Another category of life that the U.S. Supreme Court deals with is in the area of abortion rights. This issue falls under the *procedural due process of civil law.*

A person is deprived of liberty under *procedural due process of criminal law* when he or she is sent to prison. A person who is already in prison can have time off for good behavior taken away. There is also the deprivation of the conditional liberty of probation and parole. (Probation is the suspension of time remaining in the sentence of a convicted offender. To have it remain in effect, he or she must maintain good behavior and visit a probation officer regularly. Parole is the conditional release of a prisoner from the remaining jail sentence.)

Under *procedural due process of civil law,* a person could lose his or her liberty by being placed in a mental institution. This was the situation at issue in the case of *O'Connor* v. *Donaldson* (1975). Kenneth Donaldson had been in a mental hospital for fifteen years. But he had not been receiving any treatment for his mental illness. The patient brought suit. A lower court ruled that if the patient was not receiving treatment and did not represent a danger to himself or others, he could not be held against his will. This was a violation of his constitutional right to due process of law. The U.S. Supreme Court ruled that a person could not be held indefinitely just because mental illness was involved. Otherwise, it would be a loss of liberty without due process.

When it comes to the deprivation of property, there needs to be an understanding of what property is. In general, property is anything that a person has control over. This ranges from the ownership of small items that could be hidden in a pocket or purse to the ownership of a car, a house, or the side of a mountain.

Years ago—and then only briefly—there were many other types of things that were thought of as property. These included a government job, welfare benefits, Social Security disability payments, even a driver's license.

Ideas began to change about the time of *Bishop* v. *Wood* (1976). This case dealt with a police officer who had been let go from his job. He sought to get his job back on the basis that it was his property. The U.S. Supreme Court ruled that "the federal court is not the appropriate forum [place] in which to review the multitude of personnel decisions that are made daily by public agencies."

Today, *property* is often defined as a "state-created entitlement." The overall effect of this is that the rules for what makes up property are more restrictive than they used to be.

## Procedural and Substantive Due Processes

The due process clauses of both the Fifth and Fourteenth Amendments apply to procedural due process of law and substantive due process of law. Substantive due process refers to the law itself. Procedural due process, on the other hand, is divided into civil law and criminal law.

## Another Look at Procedural Due Process of Law

Procedural due process of law is a set of procedures, developed over the years, to be used in specific cases. Procedural due process can probably best be seen in action in the jury trial. Procedural due process is not limited to jury trials, however. Among other things it includes contempt of court proceedings, disbarment (expulsion, or forcing out from the legal profession), and military trials.

(For a fuller treatment of procedural due process of criminal law, see Chapter 9. See Chapter 10 for a discussion of substantive due process of law.)

## Due Process in the Schools

Everyone within the United States and its territories is protected by due process. This includes not only members of the armed forces, prisoners and aliens, but also students. A chance to present one's own case is as much a part of due process for students in school as it is for everyone else in society.

Here are two cases dealing with students' rights to present their own cases that went all the way to the U.S. Supreme Court.

- In Ohio, a principal suspended a student from school for ten days for disciplinary reasons. The state court upheld his right to use this disciplinary measure. But the U.S. Supreme Court in *Goss* v. *Lopez* (1975) overturned this ruling. The Court found a difference between staying after school and a ten-day suspension. Under procedural due process, a student faced with a ten-day suspension must be allowed the "opportunity to present his side of the story." This means he must be able to have a formal hearing with possible representation by an attorney. In a less than ten-day suspension, the principal and student resolve the issue.

    (On the subject of student suspensions, there is not the same requirement for due process in an academic suspension as there is in a disciplinary suspension. Why would this be so? Because the school administration is considered to be the authority on school curriculum and student performance and grades.)
- In Florida, two students who had received a severe paddling at school sued in court. When the case was heard by the U.S. Supreme Court in *Ingraham* v. *Wright* (1977), the vote was split 5 to 4. The Court decided that the use of

physical punishment in public school does not require notice and an opportunity for the students to be heard before the punishment.

Writing for the majority, Justice Lewis F. Powell argued that there had been no need for a hearing before the paddling. However, if a lawsuit shows that the paddling was not justified, then there needs to be some compensation given. As for the cruel and unusual punishment forbidden by the Eighth Amendment, Justice Powell stated that this applied only to criminals, not to students.

Arguing for the minority, Justice Byron R. White stated that the carrying out of cruel and unusual punishment was as possible in a school as in a prison. That was no grounds for the defeat of this case. As for procedural due process, Justice White argued that the adult should talk to the young person before the paddling about why it was needed. And as for making right a wrongful paddling, that would be difficult. The physical pain had already taken place. The psychological pain might well continue.

## More About Two Educational Issues

The attitude toward the use of physical punishment by teachers in schools is changing nationwide. By 1990, such punishment had been outlawed in twenty states. This was up from only eleven states in 1987. The case for banning physical punishment is growing. Many think that conferences and counseling, taking away privileges, and making students stay after school have been found to be better ways of changing behavior.

Another issue deals with higher education. One question that sometimes arises is why out-of-state college students have to pay higher tuition than in-state students at state colleges and universities. Wouldn't this be a violation of procedural due process under the Fourteenth Amendment? Although it may at first seem wrong that people from different states are being treated differently, the reason makes perfect sense. The students and their families who

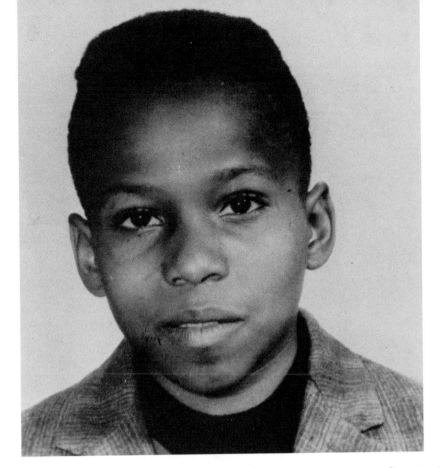

James Ingraham. In *Ingraham* v. *Wright* (1977), the Supreme Court ruled that corporal punishment in public school does not require notice and an opportunity to be heard before being punished. However, the student does have the right to sue if the punishment is excessive.

live within a state are already paying taxes to that state to help support education. People from out of state are not.

## The Importance of Fairness

In order for procedural due process of law to work, the government must do more than present an overall sense of reasonableness and fairness. The government must administer the laws fairly by applying these laws equally to all persons.

Justice Wiley B. Rutledge stated this need for fairness in procedural due process of law in just a few words. "In some respects, matters of procedure constitute the very essence of ordered liberty under the Constitution."

# Procedural Due Process of Criminal Law

"... nor be deprived of life, liberty, or property, without due process of law ..."

THE FIFTH AMENDMENT

"... nor shall any State deprive any person of life, liberty, or property, without due process of law ..."

THE FOURTEENTH AMENDMENT

Clarence Earl Gideon was a slightly built, studious-looking man who had served time in jail on four separate occasions. In the summer of 1961, Gideon was arrested for breaking into a Florida pool hall and stealing some money. At his trial in August 1961, Gideon asked to be represented by counsel, but his request was turned down by the judge.

> The Court: The next case on the docket is the case of the State of Florida, Plaintiff, versus Clarence Earl Gideon, Defendant. What says the State, are you ready to go to trial in this case?
>
> Mr. Harris [William E. Harris, Assistant State Attorney]: The State is ready, your Honor.
>
> The Court: What says the Defendant? Are you ready to go to trial?
>
> The Defendant: I am not ready, your Honor.
>
> The Court: Did you plead not guilty to this charge by reason of insanity?

---

Justice Hugo L. Black served on the Supreme Court from 1937 to 1971. He believed that all the rights listed in the Bill of Rights should protect Americans not just from actions of the national government but from state government actions as well.

The Defendant: No sir.

The Court: Why aren't you ready?

The Defendant: I have no counsel.

After a short trial, the jury returned a verdict of guilty, and the judge sentenced Gideon to five years in prison.

While Gideon was in prison, he started going to the prison library to read law books. Gideon discovered through his reading that there was a hope for him. He could submit a petition to the U.S. Supreme Court *in forma pauperis* (in the manner of a pauper, or poor person).

His petition may have been handwritten and his spelling original, but it was read with great interest. Gideon had not asked to be judged under the "special circumstances" of the "fairness doctrine" of *Betts* v. *Brady* (1942). Gideon was not claiming a "special circumstance," such as not being able to read. Clarence Earl Gideon was claiming that undergoing a trial without a lawyer violated due process of law. It was becoming clear that Gideon's handwritten petition might be an important case.

The case came up for discussion by the Supreme Court justices in one of their weekly meetings. As there were no distracting "special circumstances," the justices would be able to focus their judicial review on the decision in the *Betts* case. The justices decided to consider Gideon's petition in court.

The state of Florida and a leading Washington law firm were contacted. "In addition to other questions presented by this case, counsel are requested to discuss the following in their briefs (written argument) and oral argument: 'Should this Court's holding in *Betts* v. *Brady*, 316 U.S. 455, be reconsidered?'"

What was *Betts* v. *Brady*? This was a decision in 1942 stating in part that the lack of due process which "may, in one setting, constitute a denial of fundamental fairness, shocking to the universal sense of justice, may, in other circumstances, and in the light of other considerations, fall short of such denial." In brief, a court did not need to appoint a lawyer to represent a defendant who could not afford one.

Abe Fortas, soon to become a U.S. Supreme Court justice himself, was appointed to represent Clarence Earl Gideon. It is a great honor for a lawyer to be chosen by the Supreme Court to represent a defendant too poor to pay. Although no fee is involved, there is the chance to correct an injustice and to shape new laws.

The brief for Gideon's defense prepared by Fortas and his law firm ended with these words:

Clarence Earl Gideon in 1963. Procedural due process in serious criminal cases involving the Sixth Amendment right to counsel was applied to the state level as a result of his Court victory in *Gideon* v. *Wainwright* (1963).

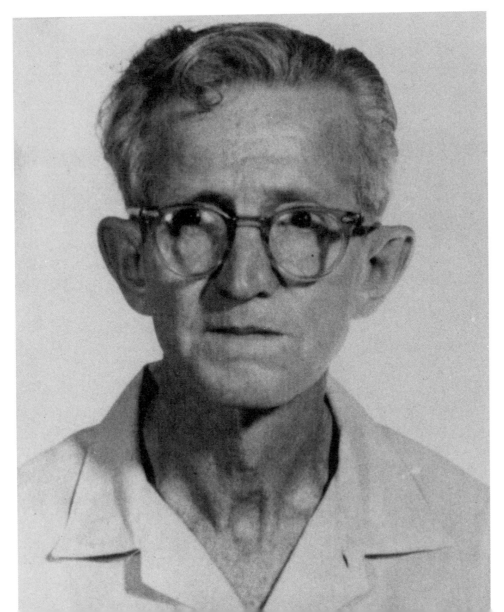

*Betts* v. *Brady* . . . has spawned [produced] twenty years of bad law. That in the world of today a man may be condemned . . . for lack of means to supply counsel for his defense is unthinkable. We respectfully urge that the conviction below [Gideon's] be reversed, that *Betts* v. *Brady* be reconsidered and that this Court require that all persons tried for a felony in a state court shall have the right to counsel as a matter of due process of law and of equal protection of the laws.

During the oral argument before the Supreme Court, Abe Fortas, a distinguished-looking man in a dark suit, stood before the nine Supreme Court justices in black robes looking down at him from the long wooden table known as a bench.

"I believe this case dramatically illustrates that you cannot have a fair trial without counsel," said Fortas.

Under our adversary system of justice, how can our civilized nation pretend that there is a fair trial without the counsel for the prosecution doing all he can within the limits of decency, and the counsel for the defense doing his best within the same limits, and from that clash will emerge the truth?

At one point, Justice Hugo L. Black leaned forward to ask why Fortas was not arguing that the Fourteenth Amendment contained all of the Bill of Rights. Fortas replied that the Court had already rejected that position so many times.

"You are saying that the right to counsel is assured by the Fourteenth Amendment whether by absorption, incorporation or whatever," suggested Justice William J. Brennan.

Two months later the Supreme Court's majority decision in *Gideon* v. *Wainwright* (1963) was read by Justice Black: "We do reconsider Betts and Brady, and we reach an opposite conclusion."

Justice Black did not use as the basis of his reasoning that the Fourteenth Amendment incorporates the Bill of Rights (a position that he had fought for during his years on the bench). Instead, he was reaching back to *Palko* v. *Connecticut* (1937). Justice Black was adapting Justice Cardozo's opinion about "the privileges and immunities that have been taken over from the earlier articles of the federal bill of rights and brought within the Fourteenth Amendment by a process of absorption."

"Not only these precedents," read Justice Black in his majority opinion to the Court, "but also reason and reflection require us to recognize that in our adversary system of criminal justice, any person haled [forced to go] into court, who is too poor to hire a lawyer, cannot be assured a fair trial unless counsel is provided for him. This seems to us to be an obvious truth." Thus the Supreme Court's decision in *Gideon* v. *Wainwright* (1963) applied the right to have counsel for serious crimes to state trials. Thus the process of making Bill of Rights protections apply to the states continued. Another guarantee of the Bill of Rights had been incorporated.

The importance of counsel for a defendant in a criminal trial had been established, and Clarence Earl Gideon had won his right to a retrial. Gideon went back to the same courthouse. This time, however, he was accompanied by a local lawyer named Fred Turner. Gideon's counsel had done his homework. This time the jury heard a far different story about what had happened that night. As a part-time helper, Gideon had a key to the pool hall. As a frequent cardplayer, Gideon always had lots of change in his pockets. The incidents of that night had not changed. It was just that this experienced lawyer was able to cast them in a far different light in order to bring out things that had been left in the dark before. When the jury filed back into the courtroom, the verdict was not guilty. Clarence Earl Gideon was now a free man.

As Justice John Marshall Harlan II would say later about a similar case: "The Court had come to realize . . . that the mere existence of a serious criminal charge constituted in itself special circumstances requiring the services of counsel at trial."

In federal trials, the Fifth Amendment has been most important in the development of law about double jeopardy and self-incrimination. In state trials, however, the due process clause of the

Fourteenth Amendment has been crucial. This due process of law was originally developed for criminal cases.

The meaning of due process first was questioned in *Murray's Lessee* v. *Hoboken Land and Improvement Co.* (1856). "The Constitution contains no description of those procedures which it was intended to allow or forbid. It does not even declare what principles are to be applied to ascertain [figure out] whether it be due process." Declaring the meaning of due process open to interpretation led to one of the most important early cases of procedural due process in criminal law. This was the case of *Hurtado* v. *California* (1884).

The defendant in this case, Hurtado, had been convicted of murder. A. L. Hart, the lawyer for Hurtado, appealed the conviction on the basis of the lack of due process. There had been no indictment from a grand jury. Wasn't that in violation of the Fifth and Fourteenth Amendments? Hart reached all the way back to Sir Edward Coke to argue that "due process of law" was the same as "law of the land."

Hurtado lost his appeal in the U.S. Supreme Court. The Court ruled that the right to a grand jury indictment did not apply to the states. In his dissenting opinion, Justice John Marshall Harlan (grandfather of John Marshall Harlan II) made a prediction. Just as the protection of the grand jury had been taken away, next it might be the protection against double jeopardy or just compensation or self-incrimination. According to Harlan, all the procedural safeguards developed in England over the centuries and used in the United States were now being called into question.

Due process, Justice Harlan observed, had been "broad enough to cover every right of life, liberty and property secured by the settled usages and modes of proceeding existing under the common and statute law of England at the time our government was founded." Could it be that the rights to a fair trial—"that due process of law which for centuries had been the foundation of Anglo-Saxon liberty—were not deemed by our fathers as essential in the due process of law prescribed by our Constitution"? Instead of there being the double protection of the Fifth and Fourteenth Amendments, now there was none. Harlan was proved right. That is just what did happen.

The certain footing that had been provided by the U.S. Constitution was replaced by a much more subjective fairness doctrine. A justice was to ask himself questions about each case in keeping with the sense of fairness that the Framers of the Constitution might have had in mind. But this ran opposite to the logic of *stare decisis,* the building on established precedent in law. "The law is not the place for the artist or poet," Justice Oliver Wendell Holmes had once remarked. "The law is the calling of thinkers."

In 1947, the case of *Adamson* v. *California* brought to light a prosecutor who had made belittling comments to the jury about the murder defendant's not taking the witness stand. It was an issue that recalled the decision in the case of *Twining* v. *New Jersey* (1908). The case of *Twining* had set a precedent. According to the Supreme Court's decision in the *Twining* case, the Fourteenth Amendment did not protect a person's right against forced self-incrimination on the state level. In a 5-to-4 decision, the justices in *Adamson* found that the defendant had received a fair trial. According to the Court, comments by judges and prosecutors on the failure of a defendant to take the stand in a state trial do not violate the Fourteenth Amendment's due process clause. Adamson had not been denied due process, since protection against self-incrimination did not apply in state trials.

"When evidence is before a jury that threatens conviction," ruled the majority, "it does not seem unfair to require him to choose between leaving the adverse [harmful] evidence unexplained and subjecting himself to impeachment [calling into question his truthfulness] through disclosure of former crimes."

In his dissenting opinion, though, Justice Black made a strong case for applying all of the Bill of Rights to the states. Black argued that the Court's interpretation of the Fifth Amendment prevented the prosecution from commenting on the failure of the accused person to take the stand in a *federal* criminal case. So the practice should not be permitted in *state* trials either. Black believed that *all* of the rights in the Bill of Rights applied to the states because of the Fourteenth Amendment. "I fear to see the consequences of the Court's practice of substituting its own concepts of decency and fundamental justice for the language of the Bill of Rights as its point of departure in interpreting and enforcing that Bill of Rights," reasoned Justice Black. "I would follow what I believe was the original purpose of the Fourteenth Amendment—to extend to all the people of the nation the complete protection of the Bill of Rights."

On the other hand, Justice Felix Frankfurter wrote an opinion concurring with the majority. He questioned why James Madison would have included a useless clause about due process of law in the Fifth Amendment. Frankfurter's argument was that the due process of law is featured in both the Fifth and the Fourteenth Amendments. But also in the Fifth Amendment are listed the people's right to a grand jury hearing, the prohibition against double jeopardy, and the prohibition against self-incrimination. In other words, if due process is simply a right and needed to be spelled out in both amendments, then the other rights listed in the Fifth Amendment should have been listed in the Fourteenth Amendment as well.

## The Pieces Fall into Place

Before the end of the 1960s, several rights of the Fifth Amendment had been incorporated under the Fourteenth Amendment.

- In *Malloy* v. *Hogan* (1964), the Supreme Court ruled that the guarantee against forced self-incrimination is also protected by the Fourteenth Amendment against state action.
- In 1965, the U.S. Supreme Court forbade the prosecutor or judge to say anything to the jury about the defendant not taking the stand in his own defense. The case of *Griffin* v.

*California* (1965) stated that this would be a "penalty imposed by courts for exercising a constitutional privilege."

- In *Benton* v. *Maryland* (1969), the Court's limitation of double jeopardy for states established in *Palko* v. *Connecticut* (1937) came to an end. The Court found

> that the double jeopardy prohibition . . . represents a funda-mental ideal in our constitutional heritage. . . . Once it is decided that a particular Bill of Rights guarantee is "funda-mental to the American scheme of justice," . . . the same constitutional standards apply against both the State and Fed-eral Governments.

At long last, the due process of law as set forth in the Fourteenth Amendment now applied parts of the Fifth Amendment to the states. However, the Fifth Amendment right to a presentment or indictment by a grand jury, in cases involving serious crimes that could lead to imprisonment of at least one year or even the death penalty, still does not apply to state trials. Nor does the Supreme Court hold that being prosecuted and even punished for the same crime by both a state government and the federal government violates the right to protection against double jeopardy.

According to Justice Robert H. Jackson: "Procedural due process is more elemental [basic] and less flexible than substantive due process. It yields less to the times, varies less with conditions, and defers much less to legislative judgment."

As discussed in the next chapter, substantive due process of law has gone through some even more remarkable changes during the course of its history.

# CHAPTER 10

# Substantive Due Process of Law

"... nor be deprived of life, liberty, or property, without due process of law..."

THE FIFTH AMENDMENT

"... nor shall any State deprive any person of life, liberty, or property, without due process of law..."

THE FOURTEENTH AMENDMENT

Procedural due process of law (both civil and criminal) is administering the laws fairly. Substantive due process of law deals with the content of the law itself. Substantive due process of law asks the question: Are the laws fair to begin with?

For centuries there was a growing belief in a higher set of laws. In Magna Carta it was "the law of the land." Even the Crown had to bow to this law. Later, "the law of the land" became associated with "due process of law."

Over the years, this higher law developed into a natural law. This was the social contract between those who govern and those who are governed. (The social contract, also known as a social compact, was a theory explaining the origin of society.)

During the early days of the United States, this philosophy was heard loud and clear in the Declaration of Independence. "We hold these truths to be self-evident," it declared, "that all men are

---

Justice Oliver Wendell Holmes served on the Supreme Court from 1902 to 1932. He once said of the Court, "We are very quiet there, but it is like the quiet of a storm centre." One of Holmes's most famous dissenting opinions was in the *Lochner* case of 1905. He opposed the majority's opinion, which used the liberty phrase of the Fourteenth Amendment's due process of law clause to protect business interests.

created equal, that they are endowed by their Creator with certain unalienable Rights, that among these are Life, Liberty and the pursuit of Happiness. That, to secure these rights, Governments are instituted among Men, deriving their just Powers from the consent of the governed." Thomas Jefferson, who wrote these words in 1776, "turned to neither book nor pamphlet while writing it." These ideas were present wherever thinking people gathered in colonial America.

James Madison, who wrote the Fifth Amendment thirteen years later, echoed Jefferson's words in the due process clause: "nor be deprived of life, liberty, or property, without due process of law." And seventy-nine years later in the Fourteenth Amendment, this influence is seen again, almost word for word: "nor shall any State deprive any person of life, liberty, or property, without due process of law." These are some of the most important words in the U.S. Constitution.

## A Test for the Fourteenth Amendment

One of the first tests for the due process clause in the Fourteenth Amendment came in the *Slaughterhouse* cases of 1873. After a series of bribes, the Louisiana legislature in 1867 gave a monopoly to the Crescent City slaughterhouse in New Orleans. The result was that other slaughterhouses in the city were banned. Some of those hundreds of butchers sued in the Louisiana courts. They claimed the Louisiana law violated the Fourteenth Amendment. The case reached the U.S. Supreme Court. A former U.S. Supreme Court justice argued for the butchers and against "the Monopoly." The man who had helped write the Fourteenth Amendment argued for "the Monopoly."

The U.S. Supreme Court ruled that there had been no violation of the Fourteenth Amendment because it did not deal with the right to make a living. Also, due process had not been violated since this law did not include the loss of property. The Supreme Court stated that instead of becoming involved in state regulation of business, the Fourteenth Amendment should concern itself only with the rights of former slaves.

Two of the justices who disagreed in this 5-to-4 decision were Stephen J. Field and Joseph P. Bradley. They said that the Fourteenth Amendment "was intended to give practical effect to the declaration of 1776 of inalienable rights, rights which are the gift of the Creator; which the law does not confer [give], but only recognizes." Justice Bradley went on to say that "rights to life, liberty, and the pursuit of happiness are equivalent [equal] to the rights of life, liberty, and property. These are fundamental rights which can only be taken away by due process of law."

Although Field and Bradley's dissents would later become the majority view of due process, this change would take many years. The dissents in the *Slaughterhouse* cases were to help set the stage for the lessening of government interference in business.

## The Freedom of Contracts

In 1897, the U.S. Supreme Court established the importance of substantive due process in *Allgeyer* v. *Louisiana*. This case dealt with the ability of people to buy insurance from a company located out of state. The Louisiana law in question prevented people from obtaining insurance on Louisiana property from any company not licensed in Louisiana. In this case, the justices overturned the state law on the basis that it interfered with due process. In other words, it interfered with the people's freedom to buy insurance from a company located out of state. In declaring that the Fourteenth Amendment contained "the right of the citizen to . . . enter into all contracts which may be proper, necessary and essential," the Supreme Court had promoted the importance of the freedom of contracts. The "liberty" mentioned in the Fourteenth Amendment protected freedom of contracts. The age of big business was under way. During the next forty years, the Supreme Court declared more than 180 state laws unconstitutional, in part because they violated the due process clause of the Fourteenth Amendment.

# The Age of the *Lochner* Case

The *Lochner* case began as a dispute over a state law supposedly designed to protect the health and safety of bakers. Under state law, workers in a bakery in Utica, New York, had been allowed to work no more than ten hours a day or sixty hours a week. In *Lochner* v. *The People of New York* (1905), the U.S. Supreme Court found this state law to be both a limitation on an employer's ability to do business and on a worker's ability to sell his or her services. The main result was to protect business.

"The general right to make a contract in relation to his business is part of the liberty of the individual protected by the Fourteenth Amendment of the Federal Constitution," wrote Justice Rufus W. Peckman for the majority. "Under that provision no state can deprive any person of life, liberty, or property without due process of law."

This decision provoked a dissent from Justice Oliver Wendell Holmes. He stated that a "constitution is not intended to embody a particular economic theory, whether of paternalism . . . or of laissez faire. It is made for people of fundamentally differing views."

Paternalism is the practice of exercising authority over others, such as workers, in a way suggesting that of a traditional father controlling his children. Laissez-faire, from the French words meaning "let them do as they choose," is the policy of opposing government interference in economic matters, except to maintain peace and property rights.

Justice Holmes later went on to spell out the meaning of substantive due process.

> The life of the law has not been logic; it has been experience. The felt necessities of the time . . . have had a good deal more to do than the syllogism [deductive reasoning] . . . in determining the rules by which men should be governed. The law embodies the story of a nation's development through many centuries and it cannot be dealt

with as if it contained only the axioms and corollaries [rules] of a book of mathematics. In order to know what it is, we must know what it has been and what it tends to become.

For years, the country held a hands-off attitude toward business. In addition, the Court favored property rights over individual rights when they came into conflict. However, things slowly started to change. The Great Depression of the 1930s brought demands from the voters and the states for Congress and President Franklin D. Roosevelt to pass and enforce laws regulating economic life. In the state of Washington, a minimum wage law for women was passed. When it was tested in the U.S. Supreme Court in *West Coast Hotel Company* v. *Parrish* (1937), the majority opinion had this to say: "The Constitution does not speak of freedom of contract. It speaks of liberty and prohibits the deprivation of liberty without due process of law." The Court had upheld the state of Washington's minimum wage law.

Despite a movement (especially in the Court of Chief Justice Earl Warren) toward favoring individual rights when they conflict with property rights, the influence of the decision in the *Lochner* case has never really ended. It can be seen in the 1980 decision in *Railroad Retirement Board* v. *Fritz*. In this suit, long-time retired employees protested that they should be able to receive their retirement benefits as well as Social Security benefits. They pointed out that more recently retired employees were able to. Justice William H. Rehnquist ruled for the Court that it was not really a case of substantive due process. It was simply the way in which the railroad rule was written. "The plain language . . . marks the beginning and end of our inquiry," Rehnquist concluded.

## Substantive Due Process and the Individual

Substantive due process deals with the reasonableness and fairness of laws and can be a way to limit the power of the government. But substantive due process does not only apply to a company fighting the impact of public regulation. It also has a bearing on the individual. The most important rulings in cases involving the legal principle of substantive due process of law in modern times have been in the area of personal freedoms and the right of privacy.

One early important U.S. Supreme Court case dealing with personal freedoms was *Meyer* v. *Nebraska* (1923). A public school teacher of the German language had been convicted of violating the law banning the teaching of modern foreign languages in the first through eighth grades. In overturning this conviction, Justice James C. McReynolds wrote about the meaning of the word *liberty* in the due process clause of the Fourteenth Amendment.

> Without doubt, [it] denotes [means] . . . the right of the individual to contract, to engage in any of the common occupations of life, to acquire useful knowledge, to marry, establish a home and bring up children, to worship God according to the dictates of his own conscience, and, generally to enjoy those privileges long recognized at common law as essential to the orderly pursuit of happiness by free men.

But perhaps one of the most controversial cases that the Supreme Court has ever dealt with is the abortion issue. Any mention of the case of *Roe* v. *Wade* (1973) gets passionate responses from both sides of the issue: pro-life (against abortion) and pro-choice (for the right to choose whether or not to have an abortion). It is an issue of such force as to spill over into the hushed-whisper corridors of the Supreme Court building itself. (Justice Oliver Wendell Holmes, Jr., once spoke about the atmosphere of the Supreme Court. "We are very quiet there," he said, "but it is like the quiet of a storm centre.")

Another important issue today deals with the people's right to die. In 1983 Nancy Cruzan had suffered severe brain damage in a car accident. She was being kept alive by means of a feeding tube attached to her stomach. The Cruzan family of Missouri, parents of the patient who had been in a coma for five years, brought suit in an attempt to have the life-support systems removed. In 1988 the Missouri Supreme Court denied Cruzan family's request to stop the food and water for their daughter.

The Cruzan family then appealed to the U.S. Supreme Court. The question was posed on grounds of substantive due process of law, in the framework of the "liberty" aspect of the Fourteenth Amendment. It was not looked at as a matter of privacy.

"The principle that a competent [legally fit] person has a constitutionally protected liberty interest in refusing unwanted medical treatment may be inferred from our prior decisions," stated Chief Justice William H. Rehnquist for the majority in *Cruzan* v. *Missouri Department of Health* (1990). But the Supreme Court justices voted 5 to 4 to reject the suit. Nevertheless, a person's right

The Cruzan family lost its case in *Cruzan* v. *Missouri Department of Health* (1990). The Supreme Court ruled that Missouri could require "clear and convincing" evidence that their severely injured daughter would want to die. Later that year, a Missouri judge ruled that there was such evidence.

COMBINED LIVING WILL AND
POWER OF ATTORNEY TO COMMUNICATE DECISION
TO FOREGO LIFE-SUSTAINING TREATMENT

To my family; all physicians, hospitals and other health care providers and any Court or Judge:

I, _____, residing at _____, make this instrument to formally record my decision, made after thoughtful consideration, to forego all life-sustaining treatment if I shall sustain substantial and irreversible loss of mental capacity **and**

I am unable to eat and drink without medical assistance and it is highly unlikely that I will regain the ability to eat and drink without medical assistance;

-OR-

I have an incurable or irreversible condition which is likely to cause my death within a relatively short time.

I do hereby appoint _____ or the survivor(s) of them if more than one, acting _____ my attorney(s)-in-fact
(insert "severally" or "jointly")
and authorize my said attorney(s)-in-fact to communicate this decision to my family, all physicians, hospitals and other health care providers and any court or judge. This authority is effective immediately.

Section 5-1602 of the General Obligations Law of the State of New York provides for a power of attorney to take effect upon the written declaration of a designated declarant that a specified contingency has occurred. Pursuant to the authority of that statute and in addition to the currently effective authority hereinabove provided to communicate my health care decisions, I do hereby appoint _____, or the survivor(s) of them if more than one, acting _____ my declarant. As and when my said declarant
(insert "severally" or "jointly")
shall, after making such factual investigation as my declarant deems necessary, declare in writing that

(1) I have sustained substantial and irreversible loss of mental capacity

-and-

(2) I am unable to eat or drink without medical assistance and it is highly unlikely that I will regain the capacity to eat and drink without medical assistance **or** I have an incurable or irreversible condition which is likely to cause my death within a relatively short time,

my attorney(s)-in-fact designated above shall have the further authority, pursuant to Section 5-1602 of the General Obligations Law of the State of New York, to communicate my instructions that all life-sustaining treatment (including without limitation administration of nourishment and liquids intravenously or by tubes connected to my digestive tract) shall thereupon be withheld or withdrawn forthwith, whether or not I am

An example of part of a living will.

to die as well as to have a living will were recognized by the Court for the first time. The U.S. Supreme Court ruled that Missouri could require "clear and convincing" evidence that Nancy Cruzan would want to die. In late 1990, a Missouri judge did rule that there was such evidence. Nancy Cruzan's feeding tube was removed, and she soon died.

The right to die may be relatively clear-cut, but what makes up a living will? A living will is a document that is drawn up by an individual before the decline of his or her reasoning powers. Often, there are several parts to a living will. A person may be named to make medical decisions for the individual if that person is no longer able to do so. This is called a durable power of attorney. A list of instructions is included to make the precise wishes of the person known. For example, the person may not want to be force-fed or be placed on an artificial respirator. The living will is signed by the person as well as by two witnesses.

## The Supreme Court: A "Super-Legislature"?

Finally, it might be helpful to recall how procedural due process and substantive due process differ. Procedural due process deals with fairness and proper procedures. It examines the way the government acts. Substantive due process, on the other hand, looks at the issue of fairness in a very different light. No matter how fair the procedure may be, if the substance or content of the law is unfair, then the whole process is flawed. In substantive due process, therefore, it is necessary to examine the substance of the law.

One problem in examining the substance of the law may lead to concerns about the Supreme Court itself. The Court may become what Justice Louis D. Brandeis referred to as a "super-legislature." This means that the Court not only interprets laws but also makes laws. Much of today's discussion about the Supreme Court revolves around this topic: How active a role should the Supreme Court take?

# Eminent Domain: The Government Versus Private Property

"... nor shall private property be taken for public use, without just compensation."

THE FIFTH AMENDMENT

The right to own property is very closely connected to our sense of freedom. "For a man's house is his castle," as Sir Edward Coke once wrote. Or, as William Pitt, the elder, in a speech to Parliament during the eighteenth century, put it: "The poorest man may in his cottage bid defiance to all the force of the Crown."

The house we live in, the car we drive, the clothes we wear—all these things have to do with ways in which we define ourselves. To a certain extent, we are what we own. If these things should ever be taken away from us, we are somewhat less than what we were before. "I have truly no property," observed John Locke in 1690, "in that which another can by right take from me when he pleases, against my consent."

It is in this spirit that we can read the last words of the Fifth Amendment ("nor shall private property be taken for public use, without just compensation"). Yes, the government does have the

---

According to the Fifth Amendment, the government has the right to take away private property such as a house if the property is intended for public use. The land might be used, for example, as part of a park or highway. However, the government must provide "just compensation."

**133**

right to take away private property within its jurisdiction for public use. However, the taking of private property cannot be done without paying for it.

## The Meaning and Origin of Eminent Domain

This right established in the Fifth Amendment is often referred to as *eminent domain*. The term comes from the Latin words *eminens,* meaning "rising high above surrounding objects," and *dominium,* meaning "domain." This is "the absolute and complete ownership of land" or "the territory over which dominion is exercised."

Eminent domain was an ancient right. In English law, the king had a right to enter the land of subjects and also to take over land as needed to defend the kingdom. But Magna Carta had set up a precedent for putting a limit on what the king could do. For example, Chapter 28 of Magna Carta stated that corn and food taken in the name of the king must be paid for. Chapter 29 said that knights cannot be forced to give money to pay mercenaries—soldiers for hire—to stand in for the knights guarding the king's castle. Chapters 30 and 31 forbade the seizure of freemen's carts, horses, and wood for the king's use.

Magna Carta of 1215 went through many different versions. By 1225, the document's original Chapter 39 had changed. It then stated: "No free man shall be taken or imprisoned or deprived of his freehold or his liberties or free customs, or outlawed or exiled, or in any manner destroyed, nor shall we come upon him or send against him, except by a legal judgment of his peers or by the law of the land. To no one will we sell, to no one will we deny or delay right or justice."

In 1625 this concept was also mentioned in a book by Hugo Grotius, a Dutch scholar and politician. The book was entitled *On the Law of War and Peace.* "The property of subjects is under the eminent domain of the state," wrote Grotius, "so that the state or he who acts for it may use and even alienate [take and give to another] and destroy such property . . . for the ends of public utility [benefit]. . . . But it is to be added that when this is done the state is bound to make good the loss to those who lose their property." James Madison might have been influenced by this famous book when he wrote the Fifth Amendment.

## Eminent Domain in the United States

In nineteenth-century England, the government took over land through the Lands Clauses Acts. But by far the greater application of eminent domain has been in the United States. Yet this important idea was not directly expressed but only implied in the body of the U.S. Constitution.

The topic is indirectly stated in the Constitution in Article I, Section 8. "The Congress shall have Power. . . To establish Post Offices and post Roads. . . ." And also, that the "Congress shall have Power. . . to exercise like Authority over all Places purchased by the Consent of the Legislature of the State in which the Same shall be, for the Erection [building] of Forts, Magazines [warehouses], Arsenals [places to make or store weapons], dock-Yards, and other needful Buildings."

This second statement gives the power of eminent domain to the state legislatures. It would not be until 1875 in *Kohl* v. *United States* that the U.S. Supreme Court allowed the federal government to use the power of eminent domain directly.

It was also not until almost three decades after the adoption of the Fourteenth Amendment in 1868 that the federal government placed any limits on the eminent domain exercised by the states.

## A Closer Look at Eminent Domain

Now, look again at what the Fifth Amendment says about eminent domain: "nor shall private property be taken for public use, without just compensation."

There are four key questions here that relate to the power of eminent domain: What is "private property"? What is "public use"? When is property "taken"? And finally, what is "just compensation"?

What is "private property"? The word *property* comes from the Latin word *proprius,* meaning "one's own." In Roman law, property was divided into "movables" and "immovables." In English law, property is divided into personal property and real property. "Things personal," as defined by Sir William Blackstone in *Commentaries,* "are goods, money, and all other movables which may attend the owner's person wherever he thinks proper to go." Real property in England is complicated by its long feudal past. In the United States, though, there are certain common characteristics in owning real property (land and buildings on it).

For example, in the United States one may own property for an unlimited number of years (as long as the property taxes are paid). Also, the terms are "fixed and certain" at the time of purchase. This means there are no hidden assets or debts. Land can also be given by will or inheritance to another person selected by the owner. In addition, ownership of land may include both what is on the surface, such as buildings and trees, and what is below the surface, such as water or oil. Finally, the owner has the right to sell or trade his or her property.

The answer to "What is property?" may have at first seemed straightforward. But in recent years the definition of property has broadened. In the case of *United States* v. *General Motors* (1945), it was discussed in a very different way. Property was no longer "... the physical thing with respect to which the citizen exercises rights recognized by law." Now it was viewed as a whole "group of rights inhering in [belonging to] the citizen's relation to the physical thing."

Now consider a very different explanation of property. Not everything that can be seen as giving an economic advantage is "private property." For instance, if the course of a river is moved upstream by a government dam, then the farmer downstream has less water to irrigate his or her crops. However, the farmer does not have to receive payment for any losses he or she may suffer.

In *United States* v. *Willow River Power Co.* (1945), Justice Robert H. Jackson argued against payment for a power company's loss of power output when the government raised the level of the river. It applies to the just-mentioned example of the farmer as well. ". . . Not all economic interests are 'property rights,'" wrote Jackson. "Only those economic advantages are 'rights' which have the law [in] back of them, and only when they are so recognized may courts compel others to forbear from [avoid] interfering with them or to compensate for their invasion."

What is "public use"? In the early years of the United States, the "public use" requirement of eminent domain meant that land had to be used by the public. For example, according to the U.S. Supreme Court's ruling in the case of *United States* v. *Gettysburg Electric Ry. Co.* (1896), privately owned land could be taken by the government in order to preserve the historic sites of Civil War battlefields.

Through many court cases over the years, however, this view of public use changed. By 1930, the Supreme Court was viewing public use as a legal problem. This was the opinion held in *City of Cincinnati* v. *Vester.* "It is well established that in considering the application of the Fourteenth Amendment to cases of expropriation [taking away] of private property," explained the Court, "the question what is a public use is a judicial one."

In recent years, public use has been greatly broadened to mean "of general benefit to the public." For instance, private land can be taken by eminent domain, then resold and developed by private contractors for a government urban renewal project. This first happened in 1954. Here is how Justice William O. Douglas described it in the case of *Berman* v. *Parker:*

We do not sit to determine whether a particular housing project is or is not desirable. The concept of the public welfare is broad and inclusive. The values it represents are spiritual as well as physical, aesthetic as well as monetary. . . . If those who govern the District of Columbia decide that the Nation's Capital should be beautiful as well as sanitary, there is nothing in the Fifth Amendment that stands in the way.

This was a big departure from the earlier ideas of public use. The decision in the *Berman* case boldly stated: "Once the object is within the authority of Congress, the right to realize it through the exercise of eminent domain is clear. For the power of eminent domain is merely the means to the end."

When is property "taken"? This can be clear-cut, as when land is condemned for a new courthouse. However, many of the court cases concerning the "taking" of private property relate to whether or not the property was actually "taken."

The government can also act in a way that reduces the worth of a property. In *Causby* v. *United States* (1946), the case involved military planes that ruined a farmer's ability to make a living. "Flights over private land are not a taking," ruled the Court, "unless they are so low and so frequent as to be a direct and immediate interference with the enjoyment and use of the land." The chickens on Causby's chicken farm had been so upset by the many low-flying planes that the farm was no longer productive. Consequently, it was a taking.

The *Causby* case is a situation of what is known as *inverse condemnation*. Inverse condemnation is the legal action brought by a property owner seeking just compensation for land where the taker of the property does not intend to bring eminent domain proceedings. For example, in the *Causby* case, the government may not have taken the farmland in the same manner as it might take land for a post office. Yet, the government did destroy the purpose for which the land was originally used.

There are many other times, however, when a ruling would be different. If an interstate highway were built near a person's property, for instance, there might be noisy traffic and exhaust fumes night and day. What might have once been an ideal home in a healthy setting might cease to be one. The resale value of the house would fall greatly, too. There would be far fewer people who would even consider living there.

South Street Seaport in New York City. Across the nation, some neighborhoods are restored in appearance by private companies. Other places are taken over by local governments but developed by private contractors for public use. Disputes often arise over whether property has actually been "taken" and whether the compensation has been enough.

Would this be considered a taking? Unfortunately for those who might be caught in such a situation, the answer is almost always no. Although the quality of life may have dropped sharply because of the highway, the predicament of the homeowners would probably be considered one of the hazards of modern life.

The most difficult cases of inverse condemnation to judge are when the value of the property has been lessened because of regulations. Consider this actual case that in some ways is the opposite of the house and highway illustration. A coal company owned the below-ground rights, and Mahon owned a house on the surface. A Pennsylvania law forbade damage to any street or building in the process of mining for coal. This made it impossible to mine the coal at a profit.

In this case, known as *Pennsylvania Coal Co.* v. *Mahon* (1922), Justice Oliver Wendell Holmes tried to weigh police power versus eminent domain. Police power doesn't mean simply power enforced by police officers. Its meaning is much broader. Police power is the power of the state to control personal freedom and property rights of people. The purpose of police power is to protect the public health, safety, and morals or to promote public convenience or general prosperity. "One fact for consideration in determining such limits [to regulations] is the extent of the diminution [decrease in value of the property]. When it reaches a certain magnitude [amount], in most if not all cases there must be an exercise of eminent domain and compensation to sustain the act." However, Justice Holmes found there was "no set formula" for finding the point where regulation stops and the taking of property starts.

There is something important to realize about state police power. If property is taken to protect the health, safety, welfare, or morality of citizens by the state police power, then there is no need for compensation.

## All Aboard: Grand Central in the Courts

An important case that dealt with whether or not a taking had occurred was in *Penn Central Transportation Co.* v. *City of New York* (1978). Penn Central, the owner of Grand Central Terminal in New York City, wanted to build a fifty-three-story tower over the railroad station. The city government, however, turned down the request. Its reason was that Grand Central had just been named a landmark building. The construction of the huge office tower would have made it necessary to make drastic changes to the outside of the station.

The U.S. Supreme Court decided that this was not a taking. Grand Central would still continue to be used as a railroad station. Also, there were many shops in the station that were rented out by the owner. Instead of a taking, the Court judged it to be a situation similar to zoning. (Zoning is dividing a city or town into separate sections for different uses, such as residential, business, and manufacturing.) It was something for the common good. The Court ruled: "Legislation designed to promote the general welfare commonly burdens some more than others." Besides, Penn Central had

Grand Central Terminal (lower right) in New York City was the center of an important 1978 case.

been permitted to transfer its air rights (property rights to the space above a building) over Grand Central to buildings it owned in other parts of the city.

What is "just compensation"? Just compensation means that the owner receives "the full and perfect equivalent in money of the property taken." (This was decided in 1943 in *United States* v. *Miller.*) And how is that amount determined? The rule of thumb is that it should be "market value"—that is, what a willing buyer would pay to a willing seller.

Unfortunately for the owner, sentimental value is not brought into account. For instance, suppose a house had been built by your great-grandparents and had been in the family ever since. Perhaps your family could never place a price on its value. Once gone, it would be lost forever. Priceless as this house might be to your family, it would not affect the amount of just compensation awarded. In other words, although something may pull on the heartstrings, it will leave the purse strings unmoved.

## Compensation in the United States

The forerunner of the "just compensation" section of the Fifth Amendment is Magna Carta. In this famous document, the English king gave up some of his absolute power.

During the early years of the United States, however, the government rarely offered compensation of any kind. If land was needed for a road, or a bridge, it was simply taken away from the owner.

It was not until the 1830s that someone challenged the government on Fifth Amendment grounds. A man named Barron owned a wharf that had been damaged by the city of Baltimore. The city, in fixing some streets, had made the water around his wharf too shallow for vessels to use. Barron wanted just compensation. This case went all the way to the U.S. Supreme Court. The justices decided in *Barron* v. *Baltimore* (1833) that the "due process of law" and "just compensation" spelled out in the Bill of Rights applied only to the federal government, not to state and local governments.

The issue of a state's power in cases involving eminent domain came up soon afterward in *West River Bridge Company* v. *Dix* (1848). Even with the persuasive pleading of Daniel Webster, one of the master orators of the day, the case was not viewed as a state's taking under the Fifth Amendment. Nevertheless, the case was won because of a violation of a law on contracts.

It was not until *Chicago, Burlington & Quincy Railroad Co.* v. *Chicago* (1897) that the Supreme Court read the Fifth Amendment into the due process clause of the Fourteenth Amendment. This meant that the compensation clause of the Fifth Amendment applied to the states. Many historians interpret this as the first right in the Bill of Rights to be incorporated, that is, applied to the states. This decision opened the door for judicial review by the Supreme Court of state court decisions in cases involving eminent domain. This was good news for people whose land had been taken away by state and local governments without just compensation. From then on, people were entitled to plead their cases under the due process clause of the Fourteenth Amendment.

In another case about a railroad, *Chicago, Burlington & Quincy Railway* v. *Commissioners* (1906), the Supreme Court set forth what was covered by state police power. *State police power* is a term that doesn't refer just to the power of police officers. Its meaning is much broader. State police power includes ''regulations designed to promote the public convenience or the general prosperity, as well as regulations designed to promote the public health, the public morals or the public safety.''

And in *Euclid* v. *Ambler Realty* (1926), the Supreme Court upheld a zoning ordinance to keep a Cleveland suburb strictly residential. Recently, the state police power has often been used in cases involving zoning issues.

## The Three Major Elements Today

Although the terms *zoning* and *state police power* do not appear anywhere in the U.S. Constitution, these two concepts have become very important in issues about property. In fact, it is these three elements—*eminent domain, state police power,* and *zoning*—that are used together in deciding many of the cases about property rights in the United States today.

# The Future of the Fifth Amendment

"No person shall be held to answer for a capital, or otherwise infamous crime, unless on a presentment or indictment of a Grand Jury, except in cases arising in the land or naval forces, or in the Militia, when in actual service in time of War or public danger; nor shall any person be subject for the same offence to be twice put in jeopardy of life or limb; nor shall be compelled in any criminal case to be a witness against himself, nor be deprived of life, liberty, or property, without due process of law; nor shall private property be taken for public use, without just compensation."

THE FIFTH AMENDMENT

The Bill of Rights has been the keystone of our freedoms since 1791. Since then, the U.S. Congress has proposed more than 10,000 amendments to the Constitution. That makes it seem all the more amazing that the Bill of Rights has remained intact. Not so much as a comma has been changed. Nevertheless, Supreme Court interpretations have influenced what the Bill of Rights means at different times in our history.

What does the future hold for the Fifth Amendment? Will the Fifth Amendment be able to keep up with the times as we enter the twenty-first century? Here is a survey of some of the possibilities.

## The Grand Jury System

The grand jury has served a crucial function down through the years. Has it, however, outlived its usefulness? Today, the grand jury is sometimes regarded as a thing of the past. Many view it as a weight on the efficiency of the court system.

---

The Supreme Court Building, Washington, D.C. As new justices are appointed to the Court, the Fifth Amendment will be interpreted in new ways.

Many problems certainly do exist. Sometimes prosecutors can mislead grand juries. Or prosecutors can take greater interest in their own political careers than in the furthering of justice. Without legal advice nearby, witnesses can cave in under clever questioning. The inability to cross-examine witnesses and to present a defense can handicap the person under investigation. Unofficial disclosures, or "leaks," can ruin lives and any possibility for a fair trial later.

What might be done about the problem of grand juries in this country? One possible solution would be for all states to do away with the grand jury system. More than half the states have already done so. In its place states could use the preliminary hearing with a district attorney, witnesses, a judge, the defendant, and the defendant's lawyer.

Another way of handling the problem would be to make certain changes to the grand jury system as it exists today. Here are some ideas.

- Allow lawyers to advise witnesses as they answer questions. (Currently, witnesses have to run out of the courtroom to speak with their lawyers.)
- Have judges take a more active role in the proceedings, as they do during regular trials.
- Maintain a written account of what takes place during grand jury proceedings, so if need be, the record can be set straight.
- Give more legal assistance to defendants during the grand jury process.
- Reduce the disclosures, or "leaks," of grand juries.

Finally, a possible solution could be a new amendment or a modification of the present-day Fifth Amendment. However, there has never once been a change to the Bill of Rights. To make one at this time might not only set a bad precedent but also weaken the amendment in the coming years.

## Military Trials

The branches of the armed forces are beginning to devise different missions for themselves from what they did in the past. For one thing, military personnel will be working side by side with civilians more often.

An example of this type of change in the mission of the armed forces is their role in dealing with the drug problem. Since 1981, there has been talk about using the armed forces to help stop the flow of drugs coming into the United States. As of this date, the armed forces do help gather information and track violators. In any case, military planners have thus far not wanted to become more involved. It is felt that it would detract from military training and preparedness. However, in the future, the armed forces may have to become more active in searches, seizures, and arrests.

Another example of the change is the use of U.S. troops alongside the troops of other nations. The greater the work load that U.S. military personnel share with civilians and foreign troops, the more problems are bound to develop. As a result, the number of court cases will increase. Whether these different cases will fall under the jurisdiction of the military court system, or under the civilian court system when they occur in this country, will be an issue of major importance. Look for an increase of U.S. Supreme Court decisions and judicial reviews of cases in this country attempting to define these growing areas.

## Double Jeopardy

The people's protection against double jeopardy may be more ancient than any other in the Bill of Rights. Phrases such as ''life and limb'' may be out of date. Still, the interpretations of this protection are often as recent as today's newspaper.

There is an irony in all of this. The law does not seem to be becoming clearer as more cases involving the people's protection against double jeopardy are being tried. Why should this be so?

One reason may be because in recent years several new justices have been named to the U.S. Supreme Court. This fact throws certain older cases into a state of uncertainty as the new justices may reconsider them according to their own interpretation. Some recent cases may be called into question as well. Instead of the law becoming more settled as more cases involving the legal principle of double jeopardy undergo judicial review, the law may be in the process of becoming more uncertain.

One future trend may be for the Court to respond more favorably to the prosecution than to the defense. This would be a shift away from the rights of the individual in favor of the rights of the government. If this happens on the national level, then certain states may develop double jeopardy laws that are more favorable to the individual. The states may become more protective of the individual's right against double jeopardy than is the federal government.

## Self-Incrimination

Some have felt that the *Miranda* warnings have gone too far. Instead of protecting everyone, some claim they coddle ruthless, hardened criminals. It is true that the purpose of the *Miranda* warnings is not to do away with confessions altogether. Rather, it is to protect average citizens when they find themselves thrust into the middle of an investigation. This is a stress-filled situation, regardless of how innocent or guilty someone may be. Just as people like to talk to a friend when troubles strike, it is often a great relief to have a lawyer there to help protect their rights.

Young people will continue to need special consideration in situations of possible self-incrimination. The juvenile in police custody tends to be particularly intimidated by the environment of the police station. In this situation, a trusted adult representing the young person's interests can be a great help.

One problem with the *Miranda* warnings is that young persons often do not want to speak with a lawyer. A lawyer may be viewed as being a part of "the other side." However, there may be an older person whom the young person might want to contact, speak with, and have present. If it is not a parent, then it might be a coach, or a teacher, or even a parole officer. It may become important in the future to draw up special rules for the juvenile. This may also be true for the many minority groups who do not speak English well. When a person from one of these groups is taken into custody, the police station may not have the resources or the skill to handle the situation. It may be necessary to develop new guidelines.

## Due Process of Law

Due process promises to be one of the most active areas in the future of all the amendments in the Bill of Rights.

Consider the issue of clarity in procedural due process of law. If people are expected to follow laws, then it stands to reason that the meaning of individual laws must be absolutely clear. Otherwise, laws can violate due process. This is true not only in specific laws. It is also the case with law as a system that helps people get along in the modern world.

Today, many people who are not lawyers are becoming involved with different aspects of the law. They are using their home computers to draw up wills. They are filing for uncontested divorces. They are undertaking title searches at city hall in order to save money on the legal fees charged for new mortgages. As more and more people are getting involved with the everyday aspects of law, there is a greater need for clear, simple English. As a result, words and phrases used in the past and often associated with law need to be replaced. Put simply, law demands plain English.

The most difficult issue in substantive due process remains the abortion question. In one way or another, many believe that having a child or not having a child will continue to be one of the most personal and private decisions. Yet many believe that the decision is an ethical one that concerns the whole community and so government should have a say in such decisions.

## Eminent Domain

In the United States today, eminent domain, state police power, and zoning are the three elements that go into creating the delicate balance in cases involving property rights.

In regard to zoning and economic regulations, if property owners suffer economic losses in the future due to unconstitutional situations, then they may be able to be compensated. If it is only a temporary taking, then it would only be a temporary compensation. However, if the taking is permanent, then it would be a full compensation. All in all, there will most likely be a return to the basic idea behind eminent domain.

## Conclusion

One of the most wonderful things about our Bill of Rights is that it is a living document. Interpretations of the Bill of Rights in general, and the Fifth Amendment in particular, change with the times.

The Fifth Amendment does not shrink in relevance or significance with the years. As a matter of fact, the protections against double jeopardy and forced self-incrimination are two of the most important features in our political history. Similarly, due process of law and eminent domain are two of the most important developments in our economic history. Instead of shrinking, the Fifth Amendment expands to include ideas and developments that the Framers of the U.S. Constitution and the Bill of Rights could not have even imagined two hundred years ago. The grand jury system, the military courts, the protection against double jeopardy, the right against self-incrimination, the concept of due process, the power of eminent domain—all of these important concepts need to remain with us in one form or another through the next two hundred years.

Maintaining the Fifth Amendment as a vital protector of rights for the citizens of the United States is not only a challenge for the

Fifth Amendment itself. It is also a test for the ability of the people who make new laws and the understanding of those who interpret old ones.

As Justice William J. Brennan, Jr., once said:

> We current Justices read the Constitution in the only way that we can: as twentieth-century Americans. The genius of the Constitution rests not in any . . . meaning it might have had in a world that is dead and gone, but in the adaptability of its great principles to cope with current problems and current needs.

The common task for all—not just for U.S. Supreme Court justices or others in government, but for every single one of us—is to make sure that the Fifth Amendment will continue to stay in step with the times as the future turns into the present.

# $\mathscr{I}$MPORTANT $\mathscr{D}$ATES

**1166**  King Henry II of England starts inquest known as Grand Assize of Claren-don. It was the forerunner of today's grand jury.

**1215**  King John of England and nobles sign Magna Carta. "Law of land" later becomes equated with "due process of law."

**1236**  Pope Gregory IX introduces the *ex officio* oath into England.

**1535**  English government beheads Sir Thomas More for refusing to swear to Act of Supremacy oath.

**1609**  England's Chief Justice Edward Coke champions Magna Carta. Equates "law of land" with "due process of law."

**1627**  John Selden acts for the defense in Darnel's case. Establishes use of due process in trial.

**1637**  English government arrests John Lilburne for bringing Puritan pamphlets into the country. During his trial for treason, Lilburne refuses to take the *ex officio* oath.

**1637**  Anne Hutchinson incriminates herself at her heresy trial in Massachusetts Bay Colony.

**1641**  Body of Liberties lists right against double jeopardy. First mention of double jeopardy in American law.

**1657**  John Lilburne dies in prison.

**1683**  Charter of Liberties and Privileges records use of inquest. First inquests held in the colony of New York.

**1692**  Witchcraft trials in Salem, Massachusetts, claim nineteen lives.

**1776**  Declaration of Independence is issued.

**1781**  British surrender to Americans at Yorktown. Independence is won.

**1787**  Constitutional Convention closes in Philadelphia. George Mason calls for a Bill of Rights.

**1789**  James Madison writes Bill of Rights.

**1791**  Bill of Rights is ratified.

**1803**  Supreme Court overturns law of Congress for first time in the case of *Marbury* v. *Madison*.

**1833**  Court rules due process and just compensation of Fifth Amendment only apply to federal government (*Barron*).

**1856**  Court deals with concept of due process for first time in the case of *Murray's Lessee* v. *Hoboken Land and Improvement Co.*

**1857** In the case of *Dred Scott* v. *Sandford*, the Court maintains that African Americans remain property in slave states and overrules Congress.

**1868** Fourteenth Amendment prohibits the states from denying any person of "life, liberty, or property, without due process of law."

**1875** Federal government uses power of eminent domain (*Kohl*).

**1884** The Court weakens due process in criminal trials in the case of *Hurtado* v. *California*.

**1905** In *Lochner* v. *The People of New York*, the Court's decision intends to protect employees but ends up protecting business.

**1908** In the case of *Twining* v. *New Jersey*, the Court states Fifth Amendment does not prevent a state from forcing a person to testify.

**1933** England abandons use of grand jury system.

**1937** The Supreme Court refuses to require states to adopt double jeopardy clause in the Bill of Rights. The case of *Palko* v. *Connecticut* leads to the incorporation of individual rights on case-by-case basis.

**1937** Wage contract in *West Coast Hotel Company* v. *Parrish* leads to national minimum wage law.

**1942** In the case of *Betts* v. *Brady*, the Court states due process changes in different situations. Allows defendant to go to trial without a lawyer.

**1950** Congress presents military with Uniform Code of Military Justice. The UCMJ is the law book for military trials.

**1950–54** Joseph McCarthy conducts Senate hearings to drive Communists out of federal government.

**1954** Private contractors develop private land for public use (*Berman*). Expands scope of eminent domain.

**1959** The Court decides in *Bartkus* v. *Illinois* that protection against double jeopardy did not apply if different governments (federal and state) prosecuted.

**1963** Court guarantees every defendant in criminal case will be provided with a lawyer. This decision occurs in the case of *Gideon* v. *Wainwright*.

**1964** In the case of *Malloy* v. *Hogan*, the Court applies guarantee against self-incrimination of Fourteenth Amendment to states.

**1964** In the case of *Escobedo* v. *Illinois*, the Court rules that a confession by a person in custody cannot be used as evidence.

**1966** In the case of *Miranda* v. *Arizona*, the Court establishes the *Miranda* warnings as basic protection for defendants taken into custody.

**1967**   Military Court of Appeals rules *Miranda* warnings also apply to military.

**1969**   The Supreme Court overturns the decision in the 1937 *Palko* case and decides that double jeopardy pertains to both state and federal governments. The decision is made in the case of *Benton* v. *Maryland.*

**1973**   Court rules on abortion issue (*Roe* v. *Wade*).

**1978**   The case of *Crist* v. *Bretz* deals with "when" the right against double jeopardy begins. The Court decides that during a jury trial, it begins after the first witness is sworn in.

**1990**   Court allows videotape made of drunk driver to be used as evidence at trial.

**1990**   Confession in prison to undercover officer also can be used as evidence.

**1990**   In *Cruzan* v. *Missouri Department of Health*, the Supreme Court recognizes for first time issues of right to die and the living will.

# $\mathcal{G}$LOSSARY

**amendment**   A change in the Constitution.

**appeal**   To refer a case to a higher court so that it will review the decision of a lower court.

**bail**   Money paid by the accused to gain his or her release in the period before trial to make sure he or she will show up for the trial. If the accused does not appear, he or she loses the money.

**bill of attainder**   A law pronouncing a person guilty of a serious crime without a trial.

**civil case**   A law case in which private individuals or businesses sue each other over property or money.

**common law**   Law based not on acts passed by lawmaking bodies but rather on customs, traditions, and court decisions.

**concurring opinion**   An opinion by one or more judges that agrees with the majority opinion but offers different reasons for reaching the decision.

**court-martial**   A military court called together under the authority of government and the Uniform Code of Military Justice, for trying and punishing offenses committed by members of the armed forces in violation of the Uniform Code of Military Justice.

**criminal case**   A law case involving a crime against society (such as robbery or murder), punished by the government.

**defendant**   The accused person, who must defend himself or herself against a formal charge. In criminal cases, this means the person officially accused of a crime.

**dissenting opinion**   An opinion by one or more judges that disagrees with the majority opinion.

**double jeopardy**   Putting a person on trial for a crime for which he or she has already been tried.

**due process of law**   The legal process guaranteed under both the Fifth and the Fourteenth Amendments to protect citizens from the government's stepping in and unlawfully taking away life, liberty, or property. Included in the due process concept are the basic rights of a defendant in criminal proceedings and the established rules for fair trials.

**eminent domain**   The power to take private property for public use by government or by private persons or corporations authorized to exercise functions of a public character.

**executive branch**   The branch or part of the government that carries out the laws and makes sure they are obeyed.

***ex officio* oath**  An oath to tell the truth sworn by a witness during the questioning of whom the questioner can ask whatever he wants. The person being examined does not even have to know the details of the investigation. This could result in self-incrimination.

***ex post facto* law**  A law that makes illegal an action that took place before the law was passed.

**federalism**  The system by which the states and the federal government, each has certain special powers and shares others.

**grand jury**  A group of from twelve (or sixteen in federal grand juries) to twenty-three citizens whose task is to decide whether there is enough evidence for a trial. It does not decide whether a person is guilty or not.

***habeas corpus***  The right of someone who has been arrested to be brought into court and formally charged.

**immunity**  Freedom, protection, or exemption from prosecution, penalty, or duty.

**incorporation**  The process of making Bill of Rights protections apply to the states so that people are safeguarded against state actions violating these rights.

**indictment**  A grand jury's written accusation that the person named has committed a crime.

**information**  A written accusation presented not by a grand jury but by a public prosecutor, charging a person with a crime.

**inverse condemnation**  Legal action, brought by a property owner seeking just compensation for land taken for public use, against a government or private group having the power of eminent domain. It is an action taken by a property owner where it appears that the taker of the property doesn't intend to use eminent domain proceedings.

**judicial activism**  A trend among courts or judges to expand their powers by making policy.

**judicial branch**  The part or branch of the government that interprets the laws.

**judicial restraint**  The belief that judges should have great respect for legislatures and executives, overruling their actions only when they are clearly unconstitutional.

**judicial review**  The power of the courts to review the decisions of other parts or levels of the government. A court may review the decision of a lower court and come to a different decision.

**just compensation**  Money payment that is fair to both the property owner and to the public when property is taken from the owner for public use through eminent domain.

**laissez-faire**  The doctrine that the government should allow the marketplace to operate relatively free of government restrictions and intervention, except to maintain peace and property rights.

**legislative branch**   The part or branch of the government that makes the laws.

**living will**   A document in which the signer specifies what treatments are or are not desired in the event of certain medical conditions that may occur when the signer can no longer make such decision. Such a document outlines what life-supporting treatments may be withheld or withdrawn from the signer if that person suffers an incurable or irreversible condition that otherwise would cause death in a short time.

**majority opinion**   The statement of a court's decision in which the majority of its members join.

**police power**   The power of the government to control personal freedom and property rights of people. The purpose of police power is to protect the public health, safety, and morals or to promote public convenience or general prosperity.

**precedent**   A previous decision of a court that is used as an example or powerful reason for a same or similar decision in a new case that is similar in facts or legal principles.

**preliminary hearing**   A hearing by a judge or magistrate to determine whether there is enough evidence to hold for a trial a person charged with a crime. For felony cases, the hearing is held before the issuing of an indictment. During the hearing, the government is required to produce enough evidence to establish that there is probable cause to believe that a crime has been committed and that the defendant committed it.

**presentment**   A grand jury's own written and signed accusation of a crime against someone, making it necessary for the prosecutor to issue an indictment.

**procedural due process of law**   The doctrine that the due process clauses of the Fifth and Fourteenth Amendments require that the legal processes developed over many years are fair, so that the government in all it does acts fairly in applying the laws.

**public prosecutor**   A lawyer who works for the government (such as a state's attorney or district attorney) and who tries to prove that the accused person is guilty of the crime charged.

**ratification**   Approval of an amendment to the Constitution by three-fourths of state legislatures or conventions (after the amendment has been officially proposed by two-thirds of each house of Congress or proposed by a convention called by two-thirds of the states).

**self-incrimination**   Act or words before or during a trial in which a suspect or an accused person admits some sort of involvement in a crime. The Fifth Amendment protects people against being *forced* to say they have committed a crime.

**separation of powers**   The division of the government into three parts or branches—the legislative, the executive, and the judicial.

***stare decisis*** The policy of courts to follow the rules and precedents set down in earlier judicial cases.

**subpoena** A legal order for a person to appear in court and testify.

**substantive due process of law** The doctrine that the due process clauses of the Fifth and Fourteenth Amendments require that laws be fair and reasonable in content.

**zoning** The division of a city or town into separate sections for different structural or architectural designs of buildings or for different uses, such as residential, business, and manufacturing.

# $\mathcal{S}$UGGESTED $\mathcal{R}$EADING

*The Bill of Rights and Beyond: A Resource Guide.* The Commission on the Bicentennial of the United States Constitution, 1990.

Brant, Irving. *The Bill of Rights: Its Origin and Meaning.* New York: New American Library, 1967.

Corwin, Edward S. *Constitution and What It Means Today.* Princeton, N.J.: Princeton University Press, 1958.

Cummings, Milton C., Jr., and David Wise. *Democracy Under Pressure: An Introduction to the American Political System,* 2nd ed. New York: Harcourt Brace Jovanovich, 1974.

Douglas, William O. *A Living Bill of Rights.* Garden City, N.Y.: Doubleday & Company, 1961.

Dumbauld, Edward. *The Bill of Rights: And What It Means Today.* Norman: University of Oklahoma Press, 1957.

Hand, Learned. *The Bill of Rights.* Cambridge, Mass.: Harvard University Press, 1958.

Hughes, Jonathan. *American Economic History.* Glenview, Ill.: Scott, Foresman and Company, 1983.

Kafka, Franz. *The Trial.* New York: Alfred A. Knopf, 1937.

Lewis, Anthony. *Gideon's Trumpet.* New York: Random House, 1964.

*Meltzer, Milton. *The Right to Remain Silent.* New York: Harcourt Brace Jovanovich, 1972.

Novick, Sheldon M. *Honorable Justice: The Life of Oliver Wendell Holmes.* Boston: Little, Brown and Company, 1989.

Weinberger, Andrew D. *Freedom and Protection: The Bill of Rights.* San Francisco, Calif.: Chandler Publishing Company, 1962.

# $\mathcal{S}$UGGESTED $\mathcal{F}$ILM

*Gideon's Trumpet.* Worldvision: Home Video Inc. Copyright by David Rintels, 1979.

*Readers of *The Fifth Amendment* by Burnham Holmes will find these books particularly readable.

# $\mathcal{S}$OURCES

Black, Hugo LaFayette. *A Constitutional Faith.* New York: Alfred A. Knopf, 1969.

Brant, Irving. *The Bill of Rights: Its Origin and Meaning.* New York: New American Library, 1967.

Burton, George Adams. *Constitutional History of England,* rev. ed. New York: Holt, Rinehart and Winston, 1962.

Clark, Leroy D. *The Grand Jury: The Use and Abuse of Political Power.* New York: The New York Times Book Company, n.d.

Corwin, Edward S. *The Constitution and What It Means Today.* Princeton, N.J.: Princeton University Press, 1958.

Douglas, William O. *An Almanac of Liberty.* Garden City, N.Y.: Doubleday & Company, 1954.

Dumbauld, Edward. *The Bill of Rights: And What It Means Today.* Norman: University of Oklahoma Press, 1957.

*Encyclopaedia Britannica,* 11th ed. New York: The Encyclopaedia Britannica Company, 1911.

Fellman, David. *The Defendant's Rights Today.* Madison: University of Wisconsin Press, 1976.

Friedrich, Carl J. *Constitutional Government and Democracy,* rev. ed. New York: Ginn and Company, 1950.

Garraty, John A., and Peter Gay. *The Columbia History of the World.* New York: Harper & Row, 1972.

*The Guide to American Law: Everyone's Legal Encyclopedia.* St. Paul, Minn.: West Publishing Co., 1984.

Hamilton, Alexander, John Jay, and James Madison. *The Federalist.* New York: Random House, 1937.

Hughes, Jonathan. *American Economic History.* Glenview, Ill.: Scott, Foresman and Company, 1983.

Kafka, Franz. *The Trial.* New York: Alfred A. Knopf, 1937.

Killian, Johnny H., ed. *The Constitution of the United States of America: Analysis and Interpretation.* Washington: U.S. Government Printing Office, 1987.

Levy, Leonard W. *Origins of the Fifth Amendment: The Right Against Self-Incrimination.* New York: Oxford University Press, 1968.

———, ed. *Encyclopedia of the American Constitution.* New York: Macmillan Publishing Company, 1986.

Lewis, Anthony. *Gideon's Trumpet.* New York: Random House, 1964.

McDonald, Forrest. *A Constitutional History of the United States.* Malabar, Fla.: Robert E. Krieger Publishing Company, 1982.

Mashaw, Jerry L. *Due Process in the Administrative State.* New Haven, Conn.: Yale University Press, 1985.

Meltzer, Milton. *The Right to Remain Silent.* New York: Harcourt Brace Jovanovich, 1972.

Mendelson, Wallace. *Justices Black and Frankfurter: Conflict in the Court.* Chicago, Ill.: University of Chicago Press, 1961.

Paul, Ellen Frankel. *Property Rights and Eminent Domain.* New Brunswick, N.J.: Transaction, 1987.

Rutland, Robert Allen. *The Birth of the Bill of Rights, 1776–1791.* Chapel Hill: University of North Carolina Press, 1955.

Schwartz, Bernard. *The Law in America.* New York: American Heritage Publishing Co., 1974.

Small, Norman J., ed. *The Constitution of the United States of America: Analysis and Interpretation.* Washington: U.S. Government Printing Office, 1964.

Weinberger, Andrew D. *Freedom and Protection: The Bill of Rights.* San Francisco, Calif.: Chandler Publishing Company, 1962.

# ℐNDEX OF ℭASES

## Author's Acknowledgments

For their kind assistance, I would like to thank Katherine Reickert and Francis Moulton, librarians at Green Mountain College in Poultney, Vermont. I would also like to thank Adriane Ruggiero for her careful editing, Herbert Sloan of Barnard College for his helpful review, and Richard G. Gallin for his cheerful guidance. In addition, I would like to express my gratitude to Paul R. Teetor and my father, Kenneth Booth Holmes.

## Photograph Credits

**B**urnham **Holmes**'s previous books for young adults have ranged in topics from what it's like to go through army basic training to what it's like to be a medical student in a hospital, from the world's first baseball game to the world's first Seeing Eye dog, from the mystery of an airplane crash to the mystery surrounding Nefertiti's life and death. He also wrote *The Third Amendment* for *The American Heritage History of the Bill of Rights*.

Burnham Holmes teaches writing at the School of Visual Arts in New York City and at the Community College of Vermont at Middlebury. Burnham and Vicki and their son, Ken, split their time between living in New York City and near a lake in Vermont.

**Warren E. Burger** was Chief Justice of the United States from 1969 to 1986. Since 1985 he has served as chairman of the Commission on the Bicentennial of the United States Constitution. He is also chancellor of the College of William and Mary, Williamsburg, Virginia; chancellor emeritus of the Smithsonian Institution; and a life trustee of the National Geographic Society. Prior to his appointment to the Supreme Court, Chief Justice Burger was Assistant Attorney General of the United States (Civil Division) and judge of the United States Court of Appeals, District of Columbia Circuit.

**Philip A. Klinkner** graduated from Lake Forest College in 1985 and is now finishing his Ph.D. in political science at Yale University. He is currently a Governmental Studies Fellow at the Brookings Institution in Washington, D.C. Klinkner is the author of *The First Amendment* and *The Ninth Amendment* in *The American Heritage History of the Bill of Rights*.